Praise for *Catch Me W*

"Poet and prophet, traveler in the realms between the worlds—the here and the greater there—Donna Stoneham is our guide to the landscapes and the inscapes of grief, loss, and the quickening of the human heart. Through this potent telling, she mentors and helps us renew and recover the connection with the love and spirit that never dies."
　　—JEAN HOUSTON, PhD, cofounder of the Human Potential
　　Movement and best-selling author of *The Possible Human,*
　　The Search for the Beloved, and *A Passion for the Possible*

"Whether or not you are religious, spiritual, or believe in life after death, Donna Stoneham's beautiful poems about loss and her letters to her dead mother will reach into your own grieving heart and guide you toward healing. Although *Catch Me When I Fall* is Donna's personal story, anyone who's had and lost a mother will relate to the connection and pain and will be uplifted—because Donna shows us that although death may end a physical life, it does not end a relationship."
　　—VIRGINIA A. SIMPSON, PhD, bereavement care specialist
　　and author of *The Space Between: A Memoir of*
　　Mother-Daughter Love at the End of Life

"Navigating grief is both an individual and collective experience, fraught with the vagaries of family history and unique personal struggles. This universal theme is turned over and over again in Donna's effective and honest writing. It is an intimate recollection and fearless accounting of the uncharted paths of grief, but it is also a metamorphosis, as she, and I believe her mother, discover the tenuous connection they thought they had with each other was not tenuous at all but one of strongly wrought love."
　　—CINDY EASTMAN, author of *Flip-Flops After 50: And Other*
　　Thoughts On Aging I Remembered To Write Down

"One suggestion, given my own tears, before you even crack open Stoneham's collection of poems—maybe don't start reading in a public space. I say that because even though we have our whole lives to prepare for the moment we become motherless, are we ever really prepared for, as Stoneham describes, 'the slack tide' of our ragged hearts? But persevere, and you will begin to understand what we call the restorative power of grief—how it moves with you, guides you, and then loosens its grip."

—NINA GABY, editor of *Dumped: Women's Stories of Women Unfriending Women*

"This very personal story of mother-daughter love captures the longing that never leaves us. The umbilical cord of that love is twisted by conflicting values and individuation, but unwinds again at the end of life, when mind gives way and reason steps aside to let love and longing be fulfilled. Written as a dialogue that extends even beyond death, Stoneham's masterful weave of prose and poetry is a primer on moving through sadness toward understanding and peace."

—MARY E. PLOUFFE, author of *I Know It in My Heart: Walking through Grief with a Child*

"I began reading Donna Stoneham's *Catch Me When I Fall* shortly before the one-year anniversary of my beloved mother's death. As I walked beside Donna through her own grief journey, I rode the too-familiar waves of sadness and overwhelm, of love and transcendence. With her powerful poetry and prose, Donna reminded me to look to the Universe for signs from my mom, to trust in the ultimate plan, and to honor our lost loved ones by spreading joy and positivity. I will forever be grateful for the healing power of this book."

—KATRINA ANNE WILLIS, author of *Parting Gifts*

"Amid the severance of earthly ties, walk with Donna Stoneham as she tenderly stitches and dresses the wound. This is difficult heart work which we will all have to do; here is a gracious reminder that we do not have to do it alone."

—LT. BRIAN BORT, US Navy chaplain and author of *The Strange Fish* and *Gigantic Brittle*

"Donna Stoneham's poignant collection of poetry and prose, *Catch Me When I Fall*, reminds us all—whatever our faith, whatever notions we may have about the afterlife—that our deepest relationships don't have to end when a dear one passes from this life. Comforting, uplifting, and deeply moving, this book shows us that although love's form may change with death, the conversations with those we hold most dear can continue, if only we keep our hearts open."
—BETSY GRAZIANI FASBINDER, marriage/family therapist
and author of *Filling Her Shoes*

"In *Catch Me When I Fall*, Donna Stoneham provides us with not only a roadmap to the wild country of grief but also an intimate travelogue. In poetry and letters, she documents every step of her journey, from the depths of bereft despair to the heights of transcendent communion. This book is a testament of a mighty love too strong for death to conquer."
—REV. JOHN R. MABRY, PhD, author of *Growing into God:
A Beginner's Guide to Christian Mysticism* and coauthor
of *Soul Journeys: Christian Spirituality and Shamanism
as Pathways for Wholeness and Understanding*

"This collection of poems brings to mind Kintsugi, the Japanese practice of repairing broken pottery with gold. The Japanese believe that by embracing and lovingly repairing what is broken, a deeper beauty is revealed. Stoneham has spun gold in these words to repair her fractured heart. Anyone who has had a complicated mother-daughter relationship, or is searching for closure after mother loss, will find comfort and truth in her words."
—HOLLYE DEXTER, author of *Fire Season* and *The Shift*

"Regardless of your relationship with your mother, when she passes, nothing touches your heart as deeply. To have this book as a resource for riding the waves of loss is like having the yummiest tincture for healing one's heart."
—JULIE STEELMAN, author of
Wild, Sacred Beauty

"Life comes with tangles. For many, the tangle that occurs in the mother-daughter relationship is painful and ongoing—but sometimes it can loosen, allowing a new avenue for love. Donna Stoneham taps into the deep longing that comes when her mother is trapped in her own collage of expectations and fear. Donna poignantly expresses the unfolding ability to see her mother, and I love that the transformation for Donna and her mom continues beyond her mom's time on earth."

—GAIL WARNER, author of *Weaving Myself Awake: Voicing the Sacred Through Poetry*

"The primal wound of losing a mother is something most of us will be asked to endure in our lifetimes. Donna Stoneham has given us the gift of letting us move with her over the rough ground of her own profound loss. Her poetry, and her poignant letters to and communications from her mother, invite us to descend into the darkness, let our hearts break wide open to love, and walk the hard and holy path of grief and loss as a portal to our own becoming."

—SUZANNE ANDERSON, author of *You Make Your Path by Walking: A Transformational Field Guide Through Trauma and Loss* and coauthor of *The Way of the Mysterial Woman: Upgrading How You Live, Love, and Lead*

"*Catch Me When I Fall* is a love story and a tale of metamorphosis that offers inspiration to all who suffer with wounds from our most primal relationship—with our mother. Interspersed with Stoneham's lovely poetry, this touching, beautiful memoir takes us through the storm of grief to a peaceful resolution with the awareness that a relationship can thrive beyond physical death. The relationship between Stoneham and her mother continues to transform, giving us a message of hope and healing that is eternal."

—CHERYL KRAUTER, MFT, author of *Odyssey of Ashes: A Memoir of Love, Loss, and Letting Go*

"*Catch Me When I Fall* vividly portrays the deeply personal ties that bind mothers and daughters and the heartache that Stoneham endured after her mother's passing. Her unconquerable spirit shines in her letters to her mother and in poetry that leaves the reader yearning for her to 'break free of the chrysalis of grief.' We are witnesses to her transformation. We too become better people after reading her story."

—CONSTANCE HANSTEDT, author of *Treading Water* and *Don't Leave Yet: How My Mother's Alzheimer's Opened My Heart*

"*Catch me When I Fall* is a beautifully woven, poetic tapestry of a love that ultimately transcends lifelong grieving. Donna Stoneham's soulful book is a metaphor for how a human can accept, embrace, forgive, and transform from hurt to being whole by allowing the work of divine love to carve her authentic self through the pain of forgiveness, rebirth, and finding joy."

—KYOMI O'CONNOR, author of *A Sky of Infinite Blue: A Japanese Immigrant's Search for Home and Self*

Catch
Me
When
I Fall

Published 2023
Printed in the United States of America
Print ISBN: 978-1-64742-428-2
E-ISBN: 978-1-64742-429-9
Library of Congress Control Number: 2022916984

For information, address:
She Writes Press
1569 Solano Ave #546
Berkeley, CA 94707

Interior Design by Tabitha Lahr

She Writes Press is a division of SparkPoint Studio, LLC.

Catch
Me
When
I Fall

Poems of Mother Loss
and Healing

Donna Stoneham

SHE WRITES PRESS

For my mother, Mary Ruth Stoneham Bond, who has been my way-shower on the path of forgiveness, love, and healing in this life and the next.

Thank you for the gifts of your abiding love, for your eternal presence, and for always being willing to hold my hand and catch me when I fall. I know that someday, when it's my time to leave this earth, that you will come for me, and I will hold your hand again.

I love you and I miss you,

Donna

To everything there is a season,
A time for every purpose under heaven:
A time to be born, and a time to die;
A time to plant, and a time to pluck what is planted;
A time to kill, and a time to heal;
A time to break down, and a time to build up;
A time to weep, and a time to laugh;
A time to mourn, and a time to dance;
A time to cast away stones, and a time to gather stones;
A time to embrace, and a time to refrain from embracing;
A time to gain, and a time to lose;
A time to keep, and a time to throw away;
A time to tear, and a time to sew;
A time to keep silence, and a time to speak;
A time to love, and a time to hate;
A time of war, and a time of peace.

—ECCLESIASTES 3:1-8 (NKJV)

Contents

Prologue

No relationship is more primal or formative than the bond between a parent and child. For many women, losing our mothers recrafts and remakes us. As adults, our connection with our mothers can be nurturing, traumatic, critical, appreciative, easy, or complex. Sometimes it's a combination of these characteristics and more. At least that was true for me.

When we lose our mothers, there is no unitary pathway to how we mourn and heal from such a foundational loss. Grief follows a path that is non-linear and repetitive—denial, anger, bargaining, depression, and acceptance, though not always in that order (Kubler-Ross 1969). And depending on the history of our relationship, this passage of grief may occur both before and after the death of our loved one. With each rotation we make around the spiral of grief, we are given the opportunity to heal another layer of pain, until ultimately, our lives can be transformed. That is the gift of grief if we are willing to enter its portal, surrender to its mystery, and allow it to transform us.

When my mother was alive, her children were her greatest teachers. As a Southern Baptist, fundamentalist Christian Republican, she lived her life in Texas until the age of eighty-five. She gave birth to two LGBTQ, progressive Democrat children who fled to the East and West Coasts in our early twenties. Needless to say, Mama's vision of who her children would become didn't turn out as she planned.

One summer in the early 1990s, we sat sipping sweet tea on her back porch in Lake Kiowa, Texas, passionately engaged in one of our many arguments about politics and religion. "Why on God's green earth would you support Newt Gingrich when you're our mother?" I asked Mama. "I guess it's no accident that you gave birth to two gay kids, and we were raised by an evangelical Christian mother. We must have a lot to learn from each other in this lifetime." As my words sailed over her head, Mama looked at me like I was speaking Latin, and we never again broached the subject.

In 2015, twenty-seven months before her death, Mama's dementia was progressing and she needed more care, so my wife Julie and I moved her to live near us in Northern California. Her last chapter here, at the end of her life, proved to be the most beautiful in our earthly relationship. During that time, our roles shifted. I became Mother to my mother, and she became my greatest teacher, whose tutelage only increased following her death.

As Mama's memory waned, her heart opened deeper, and kindness, which was her essence, prevailed. Her criticism and judgment of me ceased, as did mine toward her. In her final months on this earth, it was replaced by deep appreciation and the recognition that she accepted me for who I was, rather than the idealized version of who she hoped, if she kept praying, someday I'd become. Then almost as quickly as she arrived, the mother I'd longed for my whole life was gone.

As I've navigated through the spiral of grief of losing, gaining, and then having to say the ultimate goodbye to Mama over the past four years, she has become my Divine Mother, my link to transcendent love. She has been my guide in teaching me how to swim through the ocean of grief to discover a deep well of forgiveness, unconditional love, and eternal presence, which healed us both and made me whole.

In 1990, when I was thirty-three years old, I wrote this poem about Mama. At the time, I'd given up all expectations that we would ever resolve our differences or share the kind of relationship I'd always yearned for us to know. I finally acknowledged that to find inner peace and self-acceptance, I had to release that dream.

Letting Mama Go

Mama says she's tired,
depressed, and bitter.
Living in a fishbowl,
friends and past acquaintances
swim upstream,
as she gasps for air,
for contentment.
Struggling to stay buoyant,
to float with the tide of acceptance,
she drowns in the secrets of silence,
terrified the truth
would be
too much for them to bear.

Mama says she can't pray anymore,
her words fall on deaf ears.
She says the devil has his grip on her,
and she cannot escape him.
Mama fights so desperately
to mask appearances,
but she's breaking down inside.

Life hasn't been like a fairy tale.
This isn't the outcome she expected.
Not even Jesus can save her
from the truth . . .
Her children
didn't turn out
like she planned.

Mama's eyes look so tormented . . .
A frightened little girl
that everyone protected,
now forced to view the world
without assistance.
To cope,
without support.

Mama's pain is so pervasive,
it's hard to keep it clear.
Her pilgrimage beginning,
while mine is ending here.

I'll take Mama in my arms,
like a child without direction.
Our roles will shift.
I'll take her hand,
and lead her to the altar.

The day has come to separate.
I cannot make her passage.
I can offer empathy,
but she must make the journey.

Mama and I,
we've suffered hurt,
but I no longer blame her.

She gave the best she had to give,
and now, I must release her.

Life has come full circle now,
the time has come to leave her.
The peace she seeks
must come from within.
My prayers are with you, Mama.

When I wrote that poem thirty-one years ago, I had no idea that for the rest of Mama's life, learning how to let her go *and* let her in would become my most transformative spiritual quest. When my mother died four years ago, I was overwhelmed with unfathomable grief of losing the mother I'd always yearned for, and, in my late fifties, finally found.

A week after her death, I started a practice of writing Mama letters in my journal. I was shocked and mystified a few weeks later when she began responding back. Whenever I asked her a question, needed help, or was overcome with grief, I'd immediately hear her voice whispering words of comfort in my ear. I've been writing poetry since the dark depression that plagued my adolescence, so writing to Mama through my poet's pen was a natural release. I don't know how I would have weathered my passage of grief without the solace and guidance she provided in her replies.

In April of 2018, two months after Mama died, I attended a writing workshop with Amy Ferris. At the end of our first day, each student was given a tailored writing prompt. We were instructed to return the next day and read what we had written to the group. The prompt Amy gave me was "giving birth to myself."

As I struggled to write about that topic that night, I wrote a letter to Mama (page 61). That was the moment I realized that through my mother's death, I had lost my anchor to life. Now, I was being called to give birth to my most authentic self. I soon came to realize that the passage through the portal of grief would become my birth canal.

What I've discovered on my journey through the greatest loss I've ever experienced is that Mama was the perfect midwife for my delivery. Despite how much I always knew she loved me, in the final chapter of her life, she was learning how to nurture me the way I'd always needed. And she grew even more capable of doing so following her death. As a result of her guidance and support these past four years, after more than sixty years of struggle, I've grown to accept that I am enough, exactly as I am.

This book is a love song to my mother. It is also her love song to me, the daughter she ultimately accepted and grew proud of. Through its pages, it is my prayer that these words will be a healing balm, whether the person you're mourning is still on this earth or has traveled to the next.

My journey with Mama is a testament to the potency and power of love to heal, transform, and make us whole. One of the most important things she taught me is that it's never too late to transform our relationships, regardless of how hopeless we feel to resolve past trauma or how deep the sense of separation is from those we love.

Grief is a recursive act. It requires making meaning from each morsel of truth that's revealed as we circle back and round again through its mysterious, challenging spiral. For those reasons, I'm including the chronicle of poetry and letters I wrote during the four years following Mama's death. Some of the poems and letters may feel repetitive. But on my grief journey, I discovered there were many times I needed to dip my toes back into the familiar waters of sadness from which I'd recently emerged to find my bearings and take the next step.

As you read the words that follow, I wish you comfort on your journey. And I will hold the faith for you, as Mama did for me, that it is always possible to mend, regardless of how broken, bruised, or alone you may feel. As Mama would say from her heavenly perch, most of all, I wish you the gift of immeasurable love and self-compassion as you enter the mystery, heal your grief, and allow it to transform you.

November 2015

I have so many fears as we move Mama to California. How will she adjust to living in a place that's so different from Texas, the only place she's ever known? What if she doesn't adjust and she's miserable here? What if I'm not capable of taking care of her as her dementia progresses and her needs increase? What if the burden of being responsible for her becomes too much, and the boundaries I've created to stay healthy become blurred? What if everything I do to try and make her happy isn't enough and I fail to keep her safe?

Prayers for Passage

Tow-headed child
just three years old
wanders off the homestead,
searching for her mama.

Skipping down rocks
on tiny feet
in hand-me-down shoes,
oblivious she's ventured
so far away from home.

Fearless and excited,
her first journey
off the farm,
the Caprock calls her
to explore.

Sun falls to night.

In harried search
her brothers
set off

on horseback
hunting for the little girl,
now frightened and alone.

Eighty-two years pass,
the old woman prepares
to embark on a final adventure.
But this time,
the one in the saddle
is me.

Now Mother to my mother,
I pray for grace
to keep her safe.
For patience
to meet her needs.
And for compassion
to offer loving passage
as she says farewell
to all she's known,
and disembarks
in a strange
and foreign land.

February 2018

I have entered the portal I envisioned three months ago as I drifted off to sleep—the portal of the ancestors through which all the women in my lineage now have passed except for me. I am gutted by the deepest sadness I've ever experienced, yet the hollow space inside my chest is filled with a deeper knowing, a more fluid grace bathed in gentle peace, because I know that you aren't suffering anymore.

The Coming Home Place

Hi Mama,

This is the first time I've flown to Texas without you since you moved to California almost two and a half years ago. Now my task is to take your body home and bury it next to Daddy's on your beloved Texas plains.

Three weeks ago, you told us at dinner how you doubted you'd be here much longer. And when I met you at the ambulance ten days ago, the nurse in the ER asked if you knew where you were and you responded, "I think I'm in the coming home place." You obviously knew more than we gave you credit for or wanted to admit. I'm in still in shock that you are gone.

This is the longest we've not spoken in more than twenty years. My heart is broken into pieces. I ache for the touch of your soft, gentle hands and would give anything to pick up the phone and hear your sweet voice saying, "Honey, it's your Mama," as I have every single day for the past eight years. Despite your physical absence, I feel you with me every second. I sense the comfort of your angel arms around me. You keep sending signs and signals like the song "Softly and Tenderly" that just started playing on its own through my iPhone yesterday, the same song that was playing as you took your final breath.

Mama, I now understand I have entered the portal I envisioned three months ago as I was drifting off to sleep. It is the portal of the ancestors through which all the women of my lineage now have passed except for me. It was such a beautiful experience when you took your last breath and I felt Maw Maw's hand reaching down from heaven to take you home.

Thank you for revealing how our mothers who have passed before us come to retrieve us as we cross the threshold from this world to the next. It brought me such comfort to know when it's my time to release this mortal coil that you'll be the one to catch me.

This past week, I've been living in a bubble of grace. I'm in the world but not of it. It's a luminal space where I'm connected to you and to heaven, yet my body is still here on earth. I'm gutted by the deepest sadness I've ever experienced, as if you left with the biggest chunk of my heart. Yet that hollow space inside my chest is filled with a deeper knowing, a more fluid grace, an exquisite gratitude, and a gentle sense of peace because I know that you're not suffering, that you are finally free and unencumbered.

Your body was so tired and broken. Your eyes could no longer see. Your mind didn't work anymore. And now you are flying freely with the angels, and that's what I want for you.

Mama, I'm so deeply grateful for the gift of spending the last twenty-seven months of your life with you in California. The two of us completed what we came here to do in this lifetime, we healed what we needed to heal, and I have no regrets. That's something that even fifteen years ago I doubted would ever happen. My heart's deepest desire to experience the love of a nurturing mother was finally fulfilled. I pray that your dream to know the unconditional love of your daughter was realized too.

I know that you were proud of me, that you loved me with your whole heart, and that you appreciated everything I did for you. I'm sorry for the times I was impatient. I wish I hadn't been so busy, and we'd had more time to sit and chat.

But what I want most deeply to express is how much I appreciate the gift of life you gave me, and for how much you taught me about the resilience of the human spirit. You showed me how much capacity we have to change, to grow, and to love across differences. And in your final years, you taught me how to make the best of challenging situations and adapt to whatever life brings us with gratitude and grace. I could not have asked for more from a mother than what I received from you in the final chapter of your life.

Mama, I'm sorry you felt anxious and afraid sometimes, but I'm sure that's different now. You were so strong, brave, and present at the end of your life. It was an inspiration to behold.

So, rest gently now in Jesus's arms, God's good and faithful servant. Your work here is complete. Abide with me in my heart and in my memories and remind me when I'm sad that you are never far away. And Mama, since I've never lived my life without you here to guide me, please catch me when I fall.

I love you and I miss you,

Donna

The Gravity of Grief

Awakening from fitful sleep
the world is darker,
less vibrant,
lonelier,
without you in it.

Holding my hands,
one clasped tightly
around the other.
Imagining
that one is yours,
and one is mine.

Yearning to hear
your voice again,
touch your hand,
and see the smile
of appreciation
in which
you held me.

Dormant tears melting
the ice floe

stored from birth,
awaiting this day
of mother loss.
Streaming from
the deepest crevice
in my heart,
and building a bridge
to you.

Heart Broken.

Wide Open.

The cycle of life,
though logical,
brings little comfort
when pain sears
through lost limbs.

So Deep.

Then Grace sweeps in,
a coddling blanket
of unending love.
Swaddling my brokenness,
you wrap me
as an infant,
holding me close
to your heart.

Your four-legged messenger
never leaves my side.
Licking salt from my tears,
reminding me
that you are never
far away.

Four-Legged Messenger

Hi Mama,

Roxie hasn't left my side since we came home from the hospital the day you died, even to pee or be fed, unless I get out of bed and take her upstairs. She's attached like Velcro to my thigh whenever I lie down to rest.

My heart smiles when I think of how often you told the story that when she found us on the busy street on Dornan Drive four years ago, you didn't want us to keep her because of the extra responsibility having a second dog would bring. Then at least a hundred times over the next few years you admitted how wrong you were for saying that because she was the sweetest dog you'd ever met, and we were so lucky to have her.

Roxie keeps looking around the room, and I know she's sensing your spirit. I see that she's taking orders from you to stay nearby as I heal my broken heart. Thank you for her comfort. I miss you with all of my being, and I know that she does too.

I love you and I miss you,

Donna

Relaunching

Waves of sorrow
sweep across the shoreline
of my aching heart,
reminding me
of your absence.
Entreating me
to adjust
to a life
without your touch.

When despair
feels insurmountable,
a hawk swoops down
across the tree line.
Grace in motion,
reminding me
of your presence,
confirming
you are near.

This stark adjustment
from who you were

to who you are becoming,
still unfolding.

A toddler again,
you take my hand
and teach me to walk
through this rocky terrain
of different knowing,
one tiny step
forward
each day.

My broken heart,
jagged and hollow.
The brine of loss
becomes the bay
on which we launch
this sacred vessel,
that carries us forward,
anew.

Crystal waters glistening
at my feet,
reflecting the joy
of the love
in your eyes
that now,
I'm enabled to see.

Holding me in the solace
of your limitless heart,
we cast off
in new relationship,
for all eternity.

This New Air

In the stillness
of the dawning light,
I feel your arms
around me.
A radiant sea
of mother love,
submerged
in the depths of my being.

Taking on water,
struggling to breathe,
in this new air
that we've been given.

Yearning to hold your hand again,
to touch your face,
to hear your laughter,
to swim alongside you,
in the current
of your afterlife.

Yet knowing
your journey

is no longer mine,
and I must learn
to navigate
this sea of grief
without you.

This primal wound
of mother loss,
my new terrain.

The slack tide
of my ragged heart
rises to meet
the mystery
of our new bond,
as I cling to the shore
of your ever-present love.

March 2018

"You are surrounded by my love every second of each day. Even death cannot separate you from my love. Grieve, if that's what you need to do to heal, but reach out to me any time you need to chat, whenever you feel sad, or whenever you need me. I promise, I'll be there."

I AM Love

Hi Mama,

I'm deeply grateful for your kind words to me this morning at the moment I needed to hear them. As I drove to your apartment today after we returned from your memorial in Texas, my heart was so heavy with grief.

I dreaded walking alone into the apartment, still the same as the day you left it, knowing you wouldn't be there to greet me. At the same time, I longed to return, because being around your belongings brings me such comfort. I know we left your body in Texas, but your spirit is still so present and palpable here.

Wiping tears from my eyes as I pulled into the parking lot, like the wings of a prayer, your sweet voice whispered in my ear, *"Honey, it's your Mama. I know I left suddenly, and I can feel your sadness, but please take comfort in the fact that I'm not suffering anymore. Just know that I'm in a better place and in better condition than I could have ever imagined. I can see again. I can walk again. My mind even works."*

As I tuned in to your comforting words, you continued, *"Sweetie, I'm in the most beautiful place you can imagine. The love here is immeasurable. So much so, in fact, I'm capable of loving you more deeply than I could when I was there. I am more present and connected to you now than when I was alive because of the physical limitations earth imposes. I want you to know that you are surrounded by my love every second of each day. Grieve, if that's what you need to do to heal, but reach out to me any time you need to chat, whenever you feel sad, or whenever you need me. I promise, I'll be there, and I won't even lose my phone!"*

I thought of how many times I'd driven to your apartment late at night to check on you when you didn't answer my calls. Then after we hired the caregivers to give you your medicine, I remembered how often I'd called them when I tried to reach you to say goodnight so they could help you find your phone . . .

Then you said something I will hold forever as a talisman in my heart: *"Remember, sweetheart, I AM love now, so I am always with you. Even death cannot separate you from my love."*

Thank you, Mama, for reminding me that you are in a better place now. I am so thankful you didn't suffer too long and didn't have to linger. And I am deeply grateful for your steadfast love and continued communication. I'm comforted in the knowledge that even though your physical body is no longer here, your spirit still guides and protects me, helping me to weather this all-consuming storm of the deepest grief I've ever known.

I love you and I miss you,

Donna

Sitting Shiva

Dark sky weeps.

Gray clouds mask sun.

Seabirds swept
in updrafts of loss,
seeking bearings.

Trees tremble.
Mother Earth
breaks open.

Mourning winds howl
as I sit Shiva,
this time
without you.

Alone.

Whitecaps christen
this new beginning
as you walk on.

Surging to shore,
a reminder
this threshold
must be crossed.

No turning back.

In fits and starts,
surrendered
to the mystery.

Surrounded
by this sacred rain
of grace.

Treading water,
releasing the hand
I promised to hold.
Cutting the cord
that bound us.

Trusting
in your watchful eye,
traversing the tsunami
in this wretched
storm of grief.

The Angel in 324

Hunkered down,
    cross-legged,
        on your living room floor . . .

Sifting through
a century of photographs
marking moments lived,
memories made,
and hundreds of lives
you touched.

Engulfed by the beauty
of a well-lived life,
and the despondency
of loss,
two sides of the coin
in love's passage.

Discovering at least
a thousand cards
amongst the silverware,

under your bed,
in your underwear drawer.
Each filled with prayers and blessings
for marriage vows made,
and children born,
for a mother,
and two husbands
you buried.
Each one,
a milestone,
on this road
of long goodbyes.

Holding mementos
more treasured than gold . . .
Majorca pearls
I brought you from Spain,
slip through my fingers—
a string of tears,
knowing now
I will be the only one
to wear them.

A plexiglass angel,
from your dresser drawer.
The yellow "Nana" coffee mug,
chipped and stained from use,
now bubble-wrapped,
like a babe in arms
to protect it.

Conversations
with loved ones,
and the aroma
of your sourdough rolls
baking in the kitchen

comes wafting back,
and stops me cold.

Opening your closet door,
nuzzling my nose
in your orange-striped sweater,
yearning to smell
the comforting scent
of a mother's love,
and feel the warmth
of your embrace,
to mend my broken heart.

Your rocking chair sits empty,
but I take comfort
in your memory
as I disassemble your life
into boxes and bags.

Hunkered down,
  cross-legged,
    on your living room floor . . .

The Greatest of
These Is Love

Hi Mama,

Today I created a memorial card for your service next week in California. You weren't in the Golden State for long, but you made many friends while you were here who want to say good-bye, especially given your quick exit.

Mama, thank you for helping me as I struggled today to find a Bible verse to use on your memorial card. As I flipped through your well-worn Bible, I heard you whisper, *"Corinthians 13:13,"* as if you were sitting right beside me. When I looked up the verse, it was underlined, starred, and circled, in case there was any doubt. "And now these three remain: faith, hope, and love. But the greatest of these is love." That is what remains between us now, a deep, abiding love that transcends life and death.

Last night, our friend Penny came over for dinner and we lit the Shabbat candles on your altar, then she recited the Mourner's Kaddish. The Hebrew words of that prayer are beautiful and brought me great peace. I doubted at this stage of your journey that you'd object it wasn't a Baptist prayer.

This morning, as I scrolled through pictures on my Facebook feed, a meme popped up that said, "Love is all that matters." After my best friend Wally, who pretended to be my boyfriend when you came to visit me in Florida, died of AIDS, he visited me in a dream. In the dream, he said he wanted me to know that all the things we get so attached to in this life are just distractions, and in the end, the only thing that really matters is love.

Mama, since you died, I finally understand what Wally was trying to tell me. Your death has been a turning point into the deepest experience of love I've ever known. As I try and resume my life without you, please help me to learn to love more fiercely, even amidst the hatred in this disturbed and mixed-up world.

I love you and I miss you,

Donna

The Four O'Clock Hour

Each morning,
before sunrise
I awaken.

The alarm
of death's denial
blares,
rousing me
from sleep.

A heavy blanket of grief
disheveled,
twists in circles
around my heart.

The nauseous
thud of reality
strikes.

This day.

Will dawn.

Without you.

Lead weights
hanging
from the bed.
Two feet,
hesitant to land.

Groggy-eyed,
sleep-encrusted
consciousness
navigates
in luminal space,
uncertain
where I am.

Motherless child
of sixty years
flounders.
Torrents of tears
descend.

Eighteen hours
to wait
for respite,
until the next cycle
of rest
begins.

Fresh Grief

Fresh grief
sears through veins—
a sulfur burn,
attacking vital organs.

Bright skies
darken at noon,
clouding vision.

Strangers on streets
once familiar,
now distant faces.

Horns blaring,
"Move faster!"
Labored feet
inhibit movement,
or reason to care.

Past due responsibilities
pile higher,
on a stack of unsent notes
of deep appreciation.

Hunger fleeting,
yearning for sleep,
and a dream
that you're still here.

Fresh grief,
a palace of contradictions.
A hinterland between
this world of illusion
and grasping,
and the next world
of beauty and love.

Fresh grief,
the holy vessel,
enabling sacred passage
to inhabit
a clear and open heart.

I Will Never Leave You

Hi Mama,

Karen's been here for the past few days helping me pack your apartment and prepare for your California memorial. Holding two funerals in four weeks has been harder than I imagined. I don't know how I would have done this without my cousin, who's the closest thing I have to a sister, and you, a second daughter.

Every time she hears me weeping in your bedroom, she comes and pulls me away from wrapping your sweaters around my face in your closet so I can smell your scent. She'll hug me, then lead me back to the living room, where I'll sit on the floor in front of your best friend Adeline as she crochets to bind her grief. Then she'll hand me another box of letters or pictures to sort through. I've been calling Karen my "earth angel" because she knows exactly what to do or say at exactly the right time.

I felt more despondent this morning when I awakened than I've felt since you've been gone. The searing pain of missing you was so intense I didn't think that I could bear it. But once again, you came to my rescue. You must have known how much I needed you, because Mama, today was filled with extraordinary miracles and blessings!

First, thank you for the three beautiful rainbows you sent us this morning. As Karen and I sat in the living room gazing out the window sipping our tea, a gorgeous rainbow popped up across the bay over Mount Tamalpais. It was exquisitely beautiful—hues of purples, blues, pinks, and yellows—a massive half-moon of grace that lit up the rainy, gray sky. I imagined you back at your easel now that you can see to paint again, transmitting a painting from heaven!

As we watched the first rainbow arc over the sky, a second one emerged right above it. "Look, Karen," I exclaimed, pointing toward the sky, "Mama wanted to make sure there was one for us both!"

A couple of minutes later, Julie and the dogs returned from their walk. She ran over to see what we were doing by the window, and a third rainbow appeared. It was the first time in my life I'd ever seen a triple rainbow. The three of us wept, because we knew you'd sent them to comfort and remind us that you were exactly where you are meant to be, painting a masterpiece in heaven.

As if that wasn't enough, you pulled another hat trick. When Karen and I took the dogs to the park this afternoon, I couldn't get my door to lock and realized the battery in my key fob was dead. As we pulled out of the parking lot to head to the hardware store to replace it, I noticed a red semi-truck cab parked on the curb. Inscribed on back of the cab was your favorite Bible verse from Philippians, "I can do all things through Christ who strengthens me."

That message took my breath away. What were the odds of seeing the mantra that guided your life on the back of a semi-truck in Richmond, California? I know you sent that message to remind me that I'm never alone and can summon the strength to make it through my darkest days if I'll only ask for help.

The trifecta came when we entered the doors of the hardware store a few minutes later. Their radio was playing the Bette Midler song "Wind Beneath My Wings," only to be followed by Rod Stewart singing, "Have I Told You Lately That I Love You?" You wanted to make the point that the love we share is strong enough to span whatever distance stands between us.

Thank you, Mama, for your constant presence, and for always reminding me that even though I cannot hug you or see you with my physical eyes, that your spirit's still here looking after me, loving me, holding me, and helping me to navigate my grief.

I am deeply grateful for all your messages and messengers, and for all the signs and signals you've been placing in my path at the moment I most need them. And I'm especially thankful, through this grace of grief, that my heart is opening to the miracles and blessings everywhere around me.

I love you and I miss you,

Donna

The Gestation of Longing

Six weeks have passed
since I held your hand,
and you opened your eyes
to bid me farewell
one last time.

Each day clicks past,
a reverse gestation
of longing
to hear your voice,
delight in your laughter,
and act as ballast
to steady your gait
from falling.
My days of mothering you
in your last days,
now ended.
The markers of loss
slowly tick past . . .

Your birthday,
now Easter.

Friday night dinners.
Weekday treats of ethnic food
and Bay Park lunches.

Helping you find your glasses.

Filling your medicine vault.
Buying you #4012 oranges,
yogurt, and muffins for breakfast.
Holding on to the back of your scooter at Target
since you were nearly blind and couldn't see.
Fastening your seat belt when we rode in the car.
Fixing your TV.
Cleaning out your refrigerator.

Helping you find your glasses.

Picking up your clothes at the cleaners.
Getting your nails done.
Taking you to doctor's appointments.
Making sure there was cash in your purse.
Writing checks to pay your bills.

Helping you find your glasses.

Our daily morning check-ins,
And evening calls good night.
My commission
to care for you,
no longer valid.

Empty time,
at grief's direction
now consumes.
The gestation of longing
holds me captive.

Love's final responsibility,
completed,
as I try and refocus,
and learn how to live
without you.

April 2018

To give birth to myself in this new world without you, I must fully trust that life will support and sustain me and that I am worthy to thrive, not just survive. I have no idea who I'll be when I emerge from the birth canal, but I will cherish everything I learn from you, and will do my best to make you proud.

If Only I Had Known

If I'd known
the last time I brought you groceries
would be our final chance
to sit and chat,
I would have dropped everything
from my busy life,
and spent the rest
of the day
with you.

You asked me to sit and stay awhile,
but I was driven by deadlines
I now see
were unimportant.

You asked me
when I could spare the time,
if I would sit on your sofa
and look at pictures,
because you couldn't remember
people's names
or how you knew them.

If I'd known
we'd only have one chance
to sit on your couch and reminisce
about the people you loved,
I would have cancelled everything,
and spent that time with you.

If I'd known
we'd never make it to Monterey
for Mother's Day,
I'd have taken you there in December.
I'd have driven you
to my workplace
on the weekend,
since you asked
so many times
to see it.

If I'd known then,
what I know now,
I'd have been less rushed
to get back to work after lunch,
and we'd have gotten our nails done more often.

I'd have taken you to San Diego,
because you always wanted to see it.
Driven you to the outlet mall,
and bought you a new pair of shoes.
Encouraged you to plant flowers in our garden,
because you loved to touch the dirt.

I'd have relented
when you asked
if you could help us unpack boxes
when we moved to our new home,

despite the fact it would have
taken twice as long.

I'd have gone with you to jewelry class,
and sat with you
on Friday nights
to sing the hymns you loved,
rather than waiting
until vespers ended
to pick you up for dinner.

If I'd known I'd never hear your voice again,
I'd have made more recordings,
taken more videos,
asked you to tell me stories
of what it was like
to grow up in the Dust Bowl,
and if you were afraid of dying.

I'd have wondered aloud
about your unfulfilled dreams,
and how you found the strength
to bury your father,
your mother,
five brothers,
and two husbands.

I'd have asked you
how you were able
to nurture and cultivate
such a beautiful garden
of friends.

If I'd known our time together
would be so short,

I'd have made fewer plans,
worked less hours,
given you more hugs,
and called you
three times each day.

I'd have hired someone else
to run your errands,
so we had more time
to sit and chat.

My mourning,
now my resting place
without you.

I'd give anything
to have you sit with me,
and hold your hand again.

If only I had known.

Easter Hearts

Hi Mama,

We just returned from Wisconsin to visit Julie's family for Easter. I didn't feel ready to travel, but I hadn't seen our nieces and nephews since we moved you to California, so I decided to make the trip. I was afraid to stray too far from home, fearing if I left that we'd somehow lose our connection. I quickly came to see how wrong I was, as you reminded me so many times that you are always near.

The past week, I've been touched by the signs and symbols you've been sending. A week ago, as I gazed at the Golden Gate Bridge out my office window, I noticed a large red helium balloon in the shape of a heart as it wafted high in the air, bobbing between the eucalyptus tree and my window. *Where in the world did that come from?* I asked myself, quickly realizing you were the one who launched it.

On the drive to the airport to catch our flight a couple of days later, I spotted a huge heart lit up in red Christmas lights off the 101 Freeway at sunrise, another reminder of your presence. Kris and Frank picked us up from the airport in Milwaukee, and as we drove to their house, I saw the word

"LOVE" inscribed in graffiti in ten-foot-tall letters on the side of a building off the highway.

Then yesterday, as I sat in the back seat as we drove to Starbucks, the tears began falling as I thought of how deeply I missed you. As I reached across the seat to find a tissue, I spotted a heart hanging from the balcony of an apartment building just as we drove by. These were all signs and symbols you placed in my path to show me no matter where I go in this big, wide world, that you are never far away.

On the flight home, while writing in my journal, you whispered, *"Honey, I love you so much, and I want your sadness to lift so you can feel joy again. Remember, Easter is all about the promise of new life. Try and celebrate the fact that I've found my new life and I'm free from all my suffering."* Then you promised, by the end of May, this debilitating grief I've been experiencing would begin to lift.

Mama, what I've realized is how the grief of your loss is compounded by the fact that I didn't have time to prepare or tell you goodbye. When Daddy and Daddy Jack died, they were both gravely ill with cancer. We knew their days were numbered, so we were able to grieve for them before they died, which made the sadness less gripping after they passed away. In your case, we only had three days to let you go, and most of that time you were unconscious. It's the double grief of shock and loss that's brought me to my knees. Quick exits are good for those departing but are terribly hard on those they leave behind.

The second reason that losing you has been so difficult is that I'd finally found the mother I'd yearned for my whole life, and then, like some cruel twist of fate, you departed. As your mind waned, your judgments ceased, and your heart opened wider. I felt valued, appreciated, and accepted for who I was, and I hope you felt the same from me. I received the gift I'd always longed for; then in an instant, you were gone.

What I'm beginning to understand is that our relationship isn't over—it's just in a different form. I just need my body and mind to catch up and trust what I know in my heart and soul is true.

On the way home from the San Francisco airport today, we missed the exit we normally take for the Bay Bridge. As we navigated our way back to the freeway winding our way through SoMa, we ended up near Oracle Park. I looked up to see a massive tower crane holding yet another heart!

So, thank you, Mama, for making this trip with me, for all the Easter hearts you sent me, and most of all, for your ever-present love.

I love you and I miss you,

Donna

Catch Me When I Fall

Living in suspended animation—
a space between worlds.
Untethered now
from the primal bond
that nurtured
and guided
this now motherless child
for over sixty years.

Your work here,
completed.

My life
must move forward
without you.

My solace now,
the silence . . .

A hawk soaring past.
Sunlight glistening off the water.
Wrapping myself
in your fuzzy pink robe.

Draping my neck
in the blue silk scarf
you brought from Ireland,
still fragrant with your scent.

Grief recalibrates,
and deconstructs
the only way
I've known the world.

No longer here
to catch me
when I fall.

Tumbling
through the emptiness
of foreign air.

Cracked open.

Ungrounded.

Uncertain
of which steps to take
without the guidance
of your steady,
outstretched hand.

I'm Here Waiting
When She's Ready

Hi Mama,

I dreamed about you earlier this week. These moments of your presence in my dreamtime are precious gifts, then I awaken and realize that you're never coming back. In my dream, you were at your homecoming party in heaven. You were dressed in your purple quilted jacket, black linen pants, and sensible yet stylish black heels. You were always a snappy dresser.

You were catching up with friends who'd passed before you . . . your bridge club buddies and best friends Wanda and Sara Frances. You were working with room with your usual flair and style. You wanted me to know that you'd been received in your new home with open arms and to show me you were happy.

Then yesterday morning I dreamed about you again. In that dream, I saw a massive, sparkling white granite building resembling a stately museum. It was an intake center where the new arrivals in heaven check in to receive their instructions. The building rested on a vibrant green lawn with rolling hills behind it. The colors in the sky were a vibrant, shimmering palette of pinks, purples, and blues, pulsating with light and energy like a Maxfield Parrish painting.

I saw your best friend Adeline's daughter, Niki, sitting on a folding chair on the grass outside the building. Then I heard your voice rise from inside the building offering me these instructions: *"Honey, please tell Adeline I'm here waiting for her anytime she's ready. Make sure you let her know that. Tell her that it's beautiful here, there's nothing to worry about, and I'll be here to greet her."*

I had a lunch date with Adeline scheduled today that we set up when we chatted last week. Like me, she's been overwhelmed by the grief of your sudden departure. She misses her best friend and table mate and is heartbroken she never got the chance to tell you goodbye.

During our lunch, I told her about the dream and relayed your message. She took everything in, then responded, "You know, I've never believed in an afterlife, but if that's where your mother is, then that's a place I'd like to be. She was the kindest person I've ever known."

After I finished work this evening, I sat on our deck to watch the sunset. A couple of minutes later, a beautiful red-tailed hawk flew past about twenty feet away. I know it was your way of thanking me for delivering your message today to "Ida Bell," as you always called her when you couldn't remember her name. When I saw that hawk this evening circling above me, I realized that now not only can you walk, hear, think, and see again, but you can also fly!

I also know that just as you'll be waiting to greet Adeline, when it's my time to leave this earth, you'll be there waiting to greet me. And on those days when my grief is so heavy, and I'd like nothing more than to join you now, that assurance brings me such comfort.

Mama, I can't imagine anyone I know who is better suited to being a greeter in heaven, and I hope you're enjoying your new job.

I love you and I miss you,

Donna

Eight Weeks

Eight weeks ago,
I washed your lifeless body,
changed your gown,
combed your hair,
and bid your soul
farewell.
Yearning to imprint
the memory
of the comfort I felt
when holding your hand
into the contours
of my shattered heart,
I lingered at your bedside,
arms draped around your shoulders,
one last time.

A final act of love.

Eight weeks later,
I'm doing my best
to move forward.
There is a void

that will never be filled.
A loss,
that can never be replaced.
A longing,
that may never subside.

When you died,
I was reborn breech.

Now struggling to find my bearings,
I falter
as the undertow
of sadness swells,
and I crash against
these ragged
shores of grief.

Eight weeks from now,
perhaps I will be lucky,
the waters will be calmer,
and I'll be blessed by grace
of learning how to swim.

The Empty Doorway

Remembering your smiling face
peeking around the corner
of the sliding glass door.
Wide eyes twinkling
in awe of the brilliant sunset
glistening off the water.
Forever worried
when the big rains came,
we'd all be swept to sea.

I think of your hand
gesturing at the Golden Gate Bridge
across the bay
in wonder.
In your old age,
you'd forgotten
the many times you said
it wasn't ladylike to point.

Your memory,
dulled by dementia
made it easier to let go
of rules and conventions,

of how things should be,
and opened your heart
to what was.

As a child from the plains
who'd rarely seen the ocean,
you were astonished
by the magic
of the rolling surf
landing gently
on the shore below.

You gazed in amazement
as tankers and cargo ships
passed beneath us,
gasped in awe
at the great blue moon
in the autumn sky.
Your fading eyes
could only view
the contours
of its image
through the telescope
we bought
for you to see it.

But mostly,
what you reveled in
during the final months
we shared with you,
was the depth
of our rekindled
mother-daughter love.

I promised myself
I wouldn't cry today.

Surely after nine weeks,
I should be adjusting
to my life
on this perch
without you.

Yet tears still flow,
as I gaze at the empty doorway
where you once stood
in appreciation
of the beauty around us,
the meals we made,
the sleepovers we had,
and the laughter we shared.

And for the stories we told
about a president
who, despite your conservative leanings,
you found appalling,
but believed in your heart
prayer could change.

But the doorway
where you once stood
is empty now
as I sit alone,
watching
the sinking sun.

Giving Birth to Myself

Hi Mama,

It's been two months since you left us. I signed up for this writing retreat a couple of weeks after you died, thinking surely by this point, the pain of your loss would have subsided. I knew so little then about how gutted I'd still feel.

Amy Ferris, our writing teacher, gave us each a prompt to write from today before we left the workshop. The topic she gave me was "giving birth to myself." After sitting in the dark for the past two hours with a flashlight so I won't disturb Julie's sleep, I've made very little progress.

I've been wishing you were here so I could ask you what it was like to give birth, since I've never had a baby myself. I've also recently acknowledged that not having children is my biggest regret. As I've wracked my brain thinking what to write about, flashes of memory surface . . . Sitting across the table from you at Catfish Louie's twenty years ago on one of my visits to Texas when I announced that Julie and I were considering fostering a five-year-old boy.

"If we decide to move forward and everything works out, then we might be able to adopt him," I told you, hoping to hear you say, "Oh, honey, that's so exciting! You and Julie would be wonderful parents!"

That was the polar opposite of your response. With my heart in your sight, you blasted these words: *"You gave up the right to be a parent the moment you decided to be gay."* Your sharp words ripped a hole in my chest from which I doubted I'd ever recover.

I drove home in an icy silence following our lunch, while you acted like nothing happened. I ran into the guest room weeping, vacillating between rage and despair, finally acknowledging you'd never be capable of accepting me for who I was. The next morning, I packed the car and left two days ahead of schedule to come home to California, and I didn't answer your calls for a month. If it had been a decade later, despite your opposition, I'm certain that Julie and I would have become parents, one way or another.

As I reflect on that time of such deep hurt and disappointment, I am also aware of how grateful I am today. Over the past eight years, your heart opened wider, and your mind expanded in ways that enabled you to grow to love me as I am, and to finally accept Julie as your daughter-in-law. I'm delighted that the birth of Ron's children enabled you to become a grandmother at the ripe old age of eighty-one. I'm heartbroken that I allowed your homophobia and the shame it caused to lead me to internalize my own. Carrying that weight for so many years because I wanted your acceptance made me miss the window of having children when we were still young enough to be parents.

Mama, as I think about giving birth to myself, what I know from all the therapy I've completed over the last thirty years is I've learned how to reparent myself. But that is different from parenting a child or giving birth to oneself.

A few months before you died, on several occasions as I drifted off to sleep, I saw a large, dark portal in my mind's eye that beckoned me to enter. I had a premonition something big was about to happen that would radically alter my life. I had no idea at the time what I was seeing was the portal of mother loss.

The first night in the ICU as I got you settled before you started vomiting blood and lost consciousness, I remember telling you that I wished life were designed in a way that you could be my mother until the day I died, not knowing it would be our final conversation.

"*Honey,*" you responded, "*I wish life were that way too. Being your mother has been one of the greatest joys of my life.*"

I'd yearned to hear you say that for sixty years, and finally, at the end of your earthly journey, you did . . .

My memory drifts back to ten years ago at the family reunion as we sat in your Cadillac in the parking lot of the Embassy Suites in 110-degree heat. As I reached over to open the door, you grabbed my other hand, squeezed it hard in yours, looked me square in the eyes, and said, "*Honey, you know the biggest regret of my life is how I tried to kill your spirit when you were a child.*"

I was completely dumbfounded, as I never expected to hear such an admission. It was the turning point in our relationship because it created the bridge that we needed to heal our relationship in the final decade of your life. That moment paved the way for me to begin to experience the gift of a nurturing mother.

So today, Mama, when I think about what it means to give birth to myself, I know I must pass through the portal of mother loss I envisioned six months ago. I also know that certain conditions must be present to enable my delivery.

First, I no longer need forceps to be reborn. What I need is love and grace. Second, I need patience. To everything there is a season, and right now, I am in a time of holy gestation through profound and gripping grief as I adjust to my life without you. This season through which I'm passing requires me to walk with courage through the pain of one of the deepest losses I will ever face. I must move slowly and deliberately through its passage and relinquish my need to control.

Third, to give birth to myself means I must focus on cultivating the qualities you whispered in my ear a few weeks after you died when you said, "*Honey, when you're feeling low, focus on the things that are most important and sustaining. Keep your heart open and keep your sight*" *fixed on love, gratitude, hope, faith, and joy. Be present to all the beauty that's around you, instead of allowing yourself to sink into the abyss of anger, resentment, anxiety, and fear.*"

As I've reflected on those cherished words you offered, I've realized that the gestation process requires that I spend far less time listening to the news and worrying about the state of our country, and far more time seeking to be kind in all my interactions. It means continuing my practices that cultivate my connection to the divine and that help keep my tender heart open. It means crying when I need to, writing every day, and surrounding myself with people who love me and who don't try and rush my process.

The fourth thing you said I'll take with me on this journey of rebirth is the wisdom that I am enough, exactly as I am. After spending most of my life feeling I'd never measure up to your expectations, one day a few weeks ago you whispered, *"Honey, please know you are enough, exactly as you are. You are a gift from God. You make a difference in people's lives every day. So instead of focusing on what you think you lack, focus on the gifts you have and do your best to share them."* What I've come to understand is that also means doing work I love, rather than making choices from a sense of duty or obligation.

Most importantly, to give birth to myself in this new world without you, I must fully trust that life will support and sustain me and that I am worthy to thrive, not just survive. I commit to living that wisdom every day with self-compassion, believing that you and my other guides are with me each step of the way.

Mama, I trust the promise you made that you'll be here to guide me on the next stage of my journey, because the cord of love that connects us is eternal. I have no idea who I'll be when I emerge from the birth canal, but I will cherish everything I learn from you and will do my best to make you proud.

I love you and I miss you,

Donna

The New Normal

Awakening
to the sound
of your sweet laughter,
the ocean of love
in your radiant eyes
captures my aching heart.
It rocks me awake
as dawn breaks anew,
through the crack
in our bedroom window.

Stark truth strikes.

Dreams now,
the bridge to reality
that you are not returning.
That I will never hug you again,
listen to another
repeated story,
comb your hair,
eat Indian food,
enjoy our Saturday lunches.

 65

The memory
of your smooth, soft hands
cupped around mine—
a gauzy visage,
but all I have
to hold me
in this purgatory
of longing.

Traversing its contours,
struggling to walk
through the silence,
to fill the time I spent
in mothering you
to mothering me,
through the deepest loss
I've ever known.

Seventy-two days
have passed now
since you left us.
It does not feel easier,
just further away
from the last time
I held your hand.

Life moves on.
There are more distractions,
fewer calls from friends,
less tolerance
for sadness.

Caught between worlds—
the new normal.

Tears,
the way
I bind my heart
to yours,
as I navigate
the contours
of this hinterland
of grief.

May 2018

"Honey, what you're experiencing now is the center of the deepest well of grief. When you feel sad, just let the tears fall. Do little things that lift your spirits, even if you can't yet feel joy. And if you need to know I'm still there with you, just look out the window and watch for the hawk, and I promise I'll fly by and greet you."

Stay and Taste the Magic

Hi Mama,

This has been the most difficult week I've experienced since your departure. It feels like nothing is tethering me to this life anymore. It's been many years since I've struggled with depression, but that dark cloud of despair is looming again. Some days, my stomach hurts so badly, I'm doubled over in pain and can't stand up straight. I've been convinced I'll share your fate and die from a bleeding ulcer. What's disturbing is that I don't care. Life without you in the world feels colorless and flat.

This recurring stomach pain is one of many incidents in my life where the lines between us have been blurred. I've found myself in the familiar double-bind of loving you and yearning to be with you, while also craving my freedom. Having autonomy from you is something I've struggled to gain my whole life. And here I am again, a barnacle attached to your spirit, thinking these past few weeks I may even share your fate.

Three days ago, when I was at the hospital having tests to determine the cause of my pain, I mentioned to the nurse who was getting me ready for the procedures that this was the first time I'd been back in a hospital since I lost my mother. She responded, "Oh, honey, I know how hard it is to lose your mother. Mine passed away ten years ago. It will get easier, but the pain of losing your mother never really goes away, no matter how old you are."

When we got home from the hospital, my doctor called. "Donna, you're going to be okay," she said. "You have something called stress-related dyspepsia. It's not actually an ulcer, but it feels like one and we treat it just the same. I'm not surprised. You've been through a lot the last few months."

After I hung up the phone, I was ambivalent about my diagnosis. On the one hand, if I died, I'd be able to see you again. But on the other, I'd be without Julie. As I fell asleep from the residual effects of the sedation from the procedures, you whispered, *"Honey, what you're experiencing now is the deepest well of grief, and even if it doesn't feel like it, you are navigating it well. You aren't trying to run from it or escape it. You are facing it head-on and allowing it to wash through you."*

"When you feel tired," you encouraged, *"rest or take a nap. When you feel sad, just let the tears fall. Don't resist your feelings. Write them down and that will help them to move through you."*

And then you promised that by the end of this month, I'd start to regain my energy and this debilitating pain of grief would start to ease.

"But in the meantime," you said, *"do little things that lift your spirits. Go outside and plant that dahlia you bought to remember me in your garden. Get your hands in the dirt for a few minutes. Do something that makes you happy, even if you can't yet feel joy.*

"And if you need to know that I'm still with you," you said, *"just look out your window and watch for the hawk, and I promise I'll fly by and greet you."* After I awakened from my nap, I opened the blinds in our bedroom, and a red-tailed hawk flew past, just as you promised before I fell asleep.

That night, you appeared in my dream healthy and fit. I ran up and threw my arms around you, weeping tears of joy. I told you how incredibly grateful I was to see you. Then in a panic, I realized I had moved everything out of your apartment, given your furniture away, and that all of your clothes were sitting in garbage bags in our garage.

In my dream, I couldn't bear to tell you that we thought you died in February, so we'd already buried your body in Texas. I was relieved the past eleven weeks had been a nightmare and this hellish time, an illusion. Then you vanished from my dream as fast as you appeared, and I descended into gut-wrenching sadness.

When Julie came home from work, she found me in my robe, weeping in the armoire, my arms cuddling your clothes we'd saved so I could smell your scent. As she pulled me away from the armoire and embraced me, we were startled to hear the sound of your laugher.

"Oh my God," Julie exclaimed, "that's Mary Ruth!"

Stunned, I looked around the room to find the source. In the pocket of my bathrobe, I reached for my phone. There was a three-minute video playing with audio clips of your voice and pictures of your life sprinkled through. Through our tears, we were overcome with wonder.

"I've never seen this movie before. I have no idea where it came from! I certainly didn't make it. I guess it's just another one of Mama's hat tricks!" I revealed.

We finally determined that my Google pictures app had created the video from my file of your pictures on my iPhone, but I still have no idea how that happened or why it started playing at that moment. As surreal as it was to hear your once-embodied voice snickering in my pocket, it settled me, so thank you.

Today on my way home from work, as I thought about how challenging this past week has been, I remembered after Daddy Jack died when I'd come to visit you each month, you'd say, *"I guess I just have the give-ups."* That video was your way of letting me know that you were here to help me work through mine.

Then I heard your sweet voice whispering in my ear, *"Honey, I know this week's been tough for you. But please know how strong you are. I just couldn't be prouder of you for how you've weathered my loss. I'm sorry it's been so difficult, and I promise it will never feel this bad again."*

"And sweetie," you said, *"it's not your time to leave the earth. You have another twenty years or so before I'll be back to come to take your hand. You can make such a difference in people's lives between now and then. You need to write your books, help people heal, and teach them about the power of love to create a better world. And I'll be there as your guide to help you do that. I can be a lot more help to you from here than I could ever have been to you there, so let me help you. Just lean on me, sweetie, and please don't give up."*

At that moment, I looked up and saw a billboard on the freeway that said, "Taste the Magic." So, Mama, with your help, I'll try and do that more each day.

I love you and I miss you,

Donna

A Different Space and Time

There's a hole in my heart
that will never be filled.
A tether to the life I've known,
now severed.

The cord that once connected us,
now ethereal.

Jagged ends dangle . . .

Impossible now
to reattach
in physicality.

Yet, constructed of love
so deep and invincible,
it can never be destroyed.

Grief-stricken,
shuffling room to room,
inconsolable.

Lost without your laughter,
but comforted
by your presence—
palpable,
yet otherworldly.
Close,
yet far away.

Memories surface
in this gale of transition . . .

The times you crawled in bed to hold me when I wanted to die.
The ways you defended me when a man I loved eviscerated me
with his cruelty.
The arguments we had about my stringy hair and short shorts
when I was a teenager.
The time you told me that your biggest regret was how you tried
to kill my spirit when I was a child.
Then three days before you died, when you told me one of the
greatest joys of your life was being my mother . . .

Tears erupt,
a broken spigot,
at the moments
least expected.

Then you appear
as a verbal apparition,
whispering words
of comfort
in my ear.
Assuring me
you are more present now
than ever,
more capable of loving me . . .

Wiser.
Without judgment.
Lucid and clear.

Binding my heart
in the holy balm of your love,
you greet me
from another space and time.

As Beautiful as Heaven

Hi Mama,

I'm drinking a hot cup of tea from the mug you bought me a year ago when Julie and I took you to Yosemite for Mother's Day. As I read the words on the mug, "Advice from Yosemite," I imagine your sweet voice offering me its advice:

- Enjoy life's peaks and valleys
- Expand your horizons
- Be an inspiration
- See beauty all around you
- Keep a sense of wonder
- Reach new heights

As I reflect on these beautiful words of guidance, the memories of that trip are a balm of grace that soothes my aching heart on my first Mother's Day without you . . .

On our drive into the park, the trees were so tall they frightened you. You were terrified they would fall from the sky and crush us. To ease your fears, I made up a story and Julie played along. Pointing to the roadside, I said, "Mama, see those white trucks everywhere parked on the side of the road? The people who drive them are called 'danger rangers.' It's their job to cut down all the old trees so they don't fall and hurt anyone on the ground."

When we arrived at the park, I opened the trunk to set up the wheelchair we'd rented since your mobility was limited and I was worried about your knee. *"I'm not riding in that thing! I'm not crippled yet!"* you exclaimed.

By then I'd learned it was fruitless to argue with you, so we went with plan B, bundled you up in an extra coat, my gloves, and one of my hats, and bought tickets for a tour in an open-air truck so you could have a bird's-eye view of Yosemite Valley.

You were smitten with the handsome young park ranger, Nick, who served as our guide, and amazed he could remember so many facts about nature without looking at his notes. You couldn't hear a word he said but nodded in agreement every time he told us about another insect, bird, plant, rock, or tree endemic to the park.

We took you to lunch at the Ahwahnee Hotel. You were mesmerized by the grandeur of the dining room but worried we'd spent too much money. *"That's one of the best meals I've had in a long time, girls,"* you said, *"but we should have split that fish into three helpings. This lunch must have cost you a fortune."* Mama, I hope you know it was a priceless gift for me to have the chance to take you there.

Despite your failing eyesight, with binoculars you were able to glimpse the silhouettes of the waterfalls at Bridal Falls and the outlines of the climbers scaling Half Dome. *"Have those kids completely lost their minds? You had better not tell me you've ever done that!"* you exclaimed.

Mama, you didn't hesitate to let me know how my adventures made you nervous. I'm sure that backpacking alone through Europe and crewing for months at a time on sailboats in the Caribbean in my twenties caused you many sleepless nights. And you've reminded me on many occasions how upset you were when I told you I'd gone skydiving and jumped out of an airplane in my thirties. But I promise you, I'm wiser now, so you can finally relax and stop worrying.

As we left the park on Mother's Day, the three of us sat on the stone wall in front of the railing at the Tunnel View overlook with the backdrop of the valley, searching for a stranger to take our picture. You turned around, pointed at the vista behind us, and with the sparkling eyes of an eighty-seven-year-old child agape in wonder, exclaimed, *"Girls, just take a look at God's great handiwork everywhere around us. I'll bet heaven's even prettier than this."* Mama, I'm certain you've found the views in heaven even more spectacular than those we saw that day.

On our drive home, you kept insisting I turn left or we'd miss the turn for Amarillo. No matter how I tried to reassure you that we were going in the right direction as we headed west to your apartment in San Pablo, those verdant fields in central California awakened your childhood memories and called you home to the fertile farmlands of West Texas. I wish I could have found the words to reassure and console you as sundowners set in.

"That trip was one of the highlights of my life-time," you told Julie and me at least a hundred times over the next few months. I still drink tea each morning in this Yosemite mug, and when I hold it in my hands, it always brings a smile. Sharing that weekend with you in Yosemite is one of my most cherished memories too.

Mama, this year we'd planned to take you to Monterey for Mother's Day, but God had other plans. It's the first time in sixty years I can't send you flowers, take you out to lunch, or call you on your special day. My heart is broken as I grieve your loss, but with your grace and guidance, I'm getting stronger every day.

I see your face shining down from heaven watching over us, and I'm convinced that even Yosemite doesn't hold a candle to its beauty. I'm grateful that you no longer need "danger rangers" to make you feel safe and secure. I watch you climb heaven's peaks and valleys with a steady gait without the need of your cane, and I'm thankful you're no longer in pain.

I watch you shape-shift into a hawk flying above the tree line and past our windows each day checking to see how your girls are managing without you, and I am comforted by your presence. Each night at dusk, I watch you light up the flame-red sun with your eternal love, and it fills my heart with peace.

Mama, what I know now that I didn't know a year ago is that no matter how vast the distance is between us, you will never let me go.

I love you and I miss you,

Donna

The Journey of Love

The heavy blanket of grief
that bound this aged infant
slowly loosens.

Just as you promised,
the swaddling
breaks open,
and paralyzed limbs
are set free.

Gauzy tears
that blocked sharp vision
slowly dissipate.

Light cracks through
fissures of mourning,
allowing sight to return.
Colors reemerge,
contrast reappears,
after months
of flattened gray.

My heart,
still aching
from the hole
your earthly presence filled.
Its jagged edges,
cut like glass,
but smoother now,
and healing slowly
with your balm
of ethereal care.

The waves of sadness
elongate,
less violent
and aggressive now.

No longer drowning.
Learning to tread water
in the current
of this new normal.

The gift of grace
and the passage of time
integrate
the death of you,
with the life of me.

Your gentle hand
guides my passage.
Your wisdom
whispers solace
whenever I need
comfort.

You did not die.

Your presence,
now more palpable
than ever.

June 2018

A couple of months ago, you promised that the heavy grief I've been experiencing would finally begin to lift. I'm happy to report that I'm feeling a bit lighter. Sometimes, a sneaker wave hits. I calm myself by remembering to listen to the surf below and imagine it's the sound of you breathing, because that's how close you are.

The Guardian
at the Gate

Hi Mama,

A couple of months ago, you promised that the heavy grief I've been experiencing would begin to lift at the end of May. I'm happy to report that I'm feeling a bit lighter. As usual, you were right on target! What I'm finding, though, is that when I'm still and quiet, the grief returns. The waves of sadness are further apart now, rather than the tsunamis they were a month ago. But sometimes a sneaker wave hits and takes my breath away. When that happens, I calm myself by remembering what you told me a few weeks after you died in one of our chats.

"Honey," you offered, *"when you feel sad and lonely, just listen to the surf below your house and imagine that's the sound of me breathing. That's how close I am to you."* I can't tell you how much comfort that brings me or how often I stop and listen to the waves rolling on the shore at Cozy Cove a few hundred feet away. Now it's warm enough at night to crack the windows in our bedroom and I can hear the surf distinctly, like a lullaby cradling me to sleep.

The way you showed up for me today was magical, Mama. Four months ago, on the day I got the call from your caregiver that you'd fallen and were on your way by ambulance to the hospital, I was working with a photographer who was here taking photos of our vacation rental. We'd planned to open it the first of March, but after you died, I didn't have the energy to be an innkeeper.

This afternoon, four months later, our first guests arrived. As I walked Cody and Elizabeth down the outside staircase to the patio to check them in to the studio, Cody pointed up to the olive tree on our upper terrace. "Wow!" he said, exclaiming your favorite word at the end of your life.

And there she sat in all her grandeur . . . a red-tailed hawk glaring down with beady eyes at Cody, sitting stately on her feathered throne in our backyard no more than twenty feet away. I'd never seen a hawk in our yard before, so immediately I imagined it was you, our gatekeeper, sizing up our first guests to ensure you approved. I laughed as I thought about the many conversations we'd had as I tried to explain why we remodeled the bottom of our house to create a vacation rental.

"Honey," you always responded, *"why in the world would you let strangers stay in your house? I don't think that's very safe. Why can't they just get a hotel?"* No matter how often I tried to explain the concept of an Airbnb or reassure you there was a separate entrance, it always worried you.

This afternoon, when I looked up and saw that hawk, I sensed you finally understood. Tears of gratitude rolled down my cheeks as I wept in front of our guests. I explained how I'd recently lost my mother and that you sometimes came to visit me in the guise of a hawk. They probably thought I was weird, but I didn't care. As soon as the hawk gave our guests her seal of approval, she quickly flew away.

So, Mama, as I sit on the deck this evening watching the sunset fade behind Mount Tamalpais and wishing you were here to share it, I'm drawn to the sweet sound of your breathing as the waves gently land on the shore below. And I hope you're flying higher with the knowledge your girls are safe and sound, and that everything's okay.

I love you and I miss you,

Donna

Four Months Ago

Four months ago,
you left us.
Each day that passes,
I am learning more
how to live
without your physical presence.

In the time that's elapsed
since I held your hand
and you took your last breath,
my heart has broken open.

Torrents of tears
have cleansed my eyes
of all that's insignificant.

Now I see beauty
in dark and light places,
as I navigate
the gravity
of a love so deep
I'm rendered speechless.

I let go,
allowing myself
to flow gently in its current,
and drift to the shore
in its tide.

I'm discovering
how to rest
in grace so vast,
I can be without doing
for hours on end.

Gently savoring the beauty
of silhouettes in shadows,
and harmony in silence,
as prayers of gratitude
whisper through the branches
of rustling trees.

I'm discovering how to traverse
the vastness
of the winds of grief
that sweep me away
so uncontained,
and become the nest
that shelters me
until I summon
the strength to fly.

Four months have passed
since you left us.
The world is vastly different now,
but I am no longer afraid.

Each day I feel you
holding my hand

in the depths of your heart.
Trusting no matter the distance
between us,
you will never
let me go.

A Mother's Love

I don't cry for you every day anymore.
I don't think about how much I miss you
every second of each day.
But in the many moments
when I remember you,
the balm of your love
steadies and rights me
when I'm falling,
enabling me
to envision hope
in the depths of despair.

As I imagine the children crying
for their mothers at the border
now numbering at least two thousand,
I know you're watching,
showering each child
with love and compassion.
Your angel chorus,
singing lullabies of comfort to those babies,
supporting those who fight
for human rights,

who are doing our best
to dig our beloved country
out of this wretched mess.

Your love reminds me
to keep my heart open,
because judgment and animosity
will only lead us
to a deeper place of hatred.

Every morning,
I sit on my perch at the window
watching and waiting
for you to fly past.
Some days as a hawk.
On others, a blue jay.
The melody of your birdsong
compels me to listen
to the deeper wisdom
in my heart,
to the lessons you taught me,
to the memory of your warm, soft hand
I never tired of holding.

A mother's love
knows no boundaries . . .
From the scorched, brown earth
of an immigrant trail
in central Guatemala,
to an internment camp
in a desert in south Texas,
or even from heaven
through the ethers,
all the way down
to earth.

A mother's love is the link
that binds us to our shared humanity.
It's exactly
what is needed
in these times
to set us free.

Just Be Kind

Hi Mama,

You continue to amaze me with your wisdom, grace, and love. As I drove to work today, I asked you to help me understand what I didn't yet know about love. Thank you for these gems you whispered in my ear.

"Imagine living in a world," you said, *"a place where there are no egos or constructs like time—a home where there's no anxiety or fear. Envision a world where only peace and joy exist, where you long for nothing because there's no longer any separation from love. Picture a creation where love is immeasurable and infuses everything within and around you. That's what it's like here, honey,"* you said.

"Every day you make a choice what world you choose to live in, even while you're still on earth," you continued. *"You can choose love and hope, or you can choose hatred and fear."* At the moment you offered that gift, I looked up to see a bumper sticker on the car in front of me on the freeway. "Just Be Kind," it said. I imagined you in the driver's seat beaming that message, gently reminding me to pay attention.

Then I heard you whisper, *"Sweetie, this is your work for the remainder of your days on earth. Just do your best to be kind. That's the answer to everything that's wrong in your world,"* you told me. *"Just practice being kind. And every kindness you extend to others will be returned to you tenfold."* As if to reinforce your point, a truck passed a few minutes later on my right. Written in bold green letters were the words "Golden Rule Produce."

And that's what you're trying to teach me. It really is that simple, isn't it, Mama? Just be kind. Treat others the way I wish to be treated. Please continue to remind me to do that whenever I stray off the path.

I love you and I miss you,

Donna

July 2018

It was the first time I've felt anger toward you in many years, but the more I struggled to breathe and the more suffocated I felt, the angrier I became. I felt helpless to control it. I was terrified that if I allowed myself to feel those feelings, you would abandon me when I needed you most.

36,000 Feet

The azure-blue ocean
reflects the love in your eyes.
White, billowing clouds
spread your blanket of care,
inviting me to rest
when I need comfort.
Swaddling me close
in the grace of your love,
eternally enfolding.

Your body is gone,
yet your arms
embrace across eternity,
encouraging me,
always leading me home
to love.

I am no longer afraid
of turbulence
or choppy waters.
No longer plagued by anxiety

of what comes next,
because I know
you're always with me,
guiding me,
protecting me,
watching over me,
ready to catch me
when I fall.

36,000 feet
is closer than I've been to you
since you breathed your last breath,
and your eyes bid their final farewell.

Flying home from my first vacation
without needing to check on you,
ensure you are safe
and cared for in my absence,
my heart aches
with a bittersweet joy,
that you are free
to fly now,
unencumbered.

There is no one left
to wonder when
I'll be back home,
to call from the airport
and say I've arrived,
or to bring a gift
of a Larimar butterfly pendant
that would bring you
such delight to wear.

36,000 feet is a long way from heaven,
but it's the closest to you
I've been able to reach,
since you spread your wings
and reached the celestial shore.

Learning to
Breathe Again

An eight-year-old child
in a sixty-year-old body
struggles to breathe.
Lungs filled with longing,
and a grief so deep,
gasping for your presence,
slowly fading.

Flashbacks to childhood
startle from sleep.
Gasping for air
in the terror-filled night,
seeking refuge
in the safety
of her mother's arms.

Your embrace,
so tight,
she feared suffocation,
but she needed your protection.

There were two choices then—
enmeshment,
or annihilation.

More than fifty years later,
inhaling deep
the medicine
that opens the airways
to the memories
of the loneliness,
the contradictions,
the neediness,
the fear,
the longing for you to love me
for who I was,
to free my spirit,
so it could soar.

Together,
we wove the fabric
of the quilt
of our individuation
that took us years to bind,
unravel,
and finally,
to mend.

It covers me
in sadness
as you slowly drift away,
and it becomes more difficult
to grasp your presence,
remember the sound of your voice,
smell your scent,
or touch your hand.

Straining for air,
as fever chills.
My body's warning
that to save my life,
I must remember
how to breathe again.

Suffocation

Hi Mama,

I followed your instructions, and Julie and I left for vacation on the Fourth of July to the Dominican Republic. You knew that break was exactly what we needed after the most difficult four months of my life. The beaches were beautiful, and the waters of the Caribbean deeply healing. Even though you were a tee-totaler your whole life, I'd be lying if I didn't tell you how much we both enjoyed the swim-up bar.

Being on the ocean for a week was magical, but I really missed my hawk. Somehow, I just couldn't picture you as a pelican, so I was glad when we got home and noticed our hawk flying figure eights above our deck. These days, there's something about the comfort of the familiar that brings me solace.

On the flight back, I developed bronchitis, which progressed into pneumonia after we got home. The last two weeks have been brutal as I've struggled hard to breathe. I've been attached to a nebulizer four times a day when I'm not flat on my back in bed. So far, with the treatments at home, I've managed to avoid going to the hospital, even though my oxygen levels are low. I wasn't surprised I managed to get pneumonia as I remembered

Louise Hay said in one of her books that the lungs are where grief is stored.

What has surprised me are the feelings of anger that have surfaced. The other night, as I was in the middle of a coughing jag at 3:00 a.m., my gasping for air turned into a fit of resentment and anger.

It was the first time I've felt anger toward you in many years, but the more I struggled to breathe and the more suffocated I felt, the angrier I became. I felt helpless to control it. I was terrified that if I allowed myself to feel those feelings, you would abandon me when I needed you most. Choking on phlegm, I was transported back to how I felt when I was a little girl. Every night I'd make the long, scary walk from my bedroom down the hall and across the stairway to your bedroom because I was terrified of who might enter my room in the middle of the night.

I'd crawl into your side of the bed, and you'd squeeze me so hard that the two of us were fused. I felt obliterated. There was no longer a boundary between us. I know at some level, you thought you were protecting me, but I felt like a trapped animal. I had two choices then, enmeshment or annihilation. Neither one of those was a choice an eight-year-old should ever have to make.

The other night when I had those flashbacks, my sobs grew so loud and my breathing so irregular that it awakened Julie. She found a paper bag for me to breathe into, as by that point I was in the throes of a full-blown panic attack. She held me until I could catch my breath as I tried to process my feelings, and she promised me that you would never leave me. There were so many things I never shared with you that I needed to tell you when I was a child, because I feared you would blame me and withdraw your love. I knew I couldn't bear that. I needed a protector.

I am relieved you didn't leave the other night when I felt such despair. I'm beginning to trust that our love is strong enough to weather any storm. That assurance is what I've needed to help my lungs begin to clear and heal. I also realized all the grief I've carried is about more than your death, despite all the work I've done over the years in therapy to repair the breach between us and heal the trauma I experienced as a child.

Next week, we fly to Texas for our family reunion. I dread the thought of going there without you. It will be the first time in forty-two years that you won't be there. I know it will be a balm for my broken heart to see your sister and my cousins, but being there without you will be bittersweet.

So, thank you, Mama, for not abandoning me when I feel angry and for being strong enough now to allow me to feel my feelings without worrying how what I feel or say might hurt you. Thank you for promising me you'll be there at the reunion to hold my hand. And most of all, thank you for loving me uncon-ditionally, and for showing me I can trust that this is true.

I love you and I miss you,

Donna

August 2018

My lungs are clearing now, along with my vision of who we were and who we are becoming in this new relationship we share. I am learning how to breathe again, unencumbered by the cloud of neediness and suffocation that bound us together in unhealthy ways. We have entered a new partnership, one in which you can see clearly now too. And I trust from everything you've shared with me that you genuinely want me to be free, to find my wings and fly. In many ways, I was your teacher when you were on this earth. Now it seems our roles have reversed, and you are becoming mine.

Forty-Two Years

For the first time in forty-two years,
we return to gather here
without you.
Remembering the times
we sat in church,
fingers entwined,
on Sunday morning.
Me, dreading the day
that I knew in my heart
you'd be missing.

Thinking of all the years
you fetched me from the airport
in the scorching Dallas heat,
until it was no longer safe
for you to drive,
and it was my turn
to safely deliver you
into the arms of
your beloved clan
at our family reunion.

Reflecting on your excitement
when we made this trip
a year ago . . .
In your bright yellow suit,
we wheeled you
from the airplane,
helped you unpack,
and reminded you
that you were back in Texas,
and who belonged to whom.

I was afraid
you wouldn't be able
to make the trip this year,
as the travel took its toll.
But I never imagined then
that we'd be here now,
crossing the country
without you.

Last year,
before everyone departed,
your brother and your sister
called us all into a circle . . .

The siblings shared your gratitude
for the ties that bind us as a family.
For the blessing of your mother
and your brothers
who'd already traveled
home to heaven.
For God's magnificent love
that has blessed us
for generations,
before the nine of you
were four.

You are not here
to hold my hand this year,
but you will always hold my heart.
I sense that you,
your parents,
and your brothers
are circled above us now
with wings outstretched.

We stand on your shoulders,
remembering everything
you tried to teach us,
as we go forth
another year,
seeking
to emulate
your love.

The Chrysalis of Grief

The final month
of summer passes.
Gray days greet
my aching heart.
A chilling fog
looms over the bay.
Smoke fills the air,
clouding vision.

Each morning I wake,
I sense you slipping
further away.
The cocoon of grief
that held me safely
in the crook of your arm,
now fraying,
loosening,
seeking to launch me
into a world
without your presence,
and I am unready
to go.

The gossamer thread
that bound me to you,
more tenuous
and illusive.

Living a life
in gray tones
since your absence.
Seeking to fill the time
that once was yours
with meaning,
finding little energy
to move.

I sit on my perch
at the window
on Sunday morning,
watching the path
where your hawk once flew.
Replaced now by buzzards,
preying on creatures
vulnerable and small.

The strength I
thought I had
is waning.
My courage,
and all the things
that made you
proud of me,
in short supply.

If grief is measured
by the love we had,
this chrysalis of protection
you wove

for me to rest in
should be more substantial,
less permeable,
more protective.

Not long ago
you told me
to never lose faith
that you would always
be here with me.

Is this your way
of forcing me out
of my cocoon
into the world
so I can fly again,
wing by broken wing,
as only a mother can do?

Learning to Be Brave

Hi Mama,

Today marks the six-month anniversary of your death. I'm on a plane to San Antonio for Aunt Nell's 95th birthday party. I'm so sad you aren't here sitting next to me. It will be so strange to be at her celebration without her little sister. You were the youngest of the four remaining siblings, so everyone assumed you'd be the last to go.

Yesterday, I met with my spiritual director, Sandra. We hadn't spoken for six weeks, and it was a deeply revealing chat. I shared how, on that horrible night a few weeks ago, I was gasping for breath, thinking that I couldn't breathe without you. Then that feeling shifted into memories of how I felt suffocated by you when I was growing up.

I told her that Julie and I had taken the kids to Disneyland last week after our family reunion, and how Sophia had been so brave when she decided to ride the roller coaster at Space Mountain. As we stood in the queue, Sophia couldn't decide whether to go on the ride or leave. I encouraged her to trust her judgment and make her own decision, but I promised whatever she decided, I would support her.

As we approached the car to be buckled in, I said, "Honey, this is your last chance to back out if you don't want to do this." She put her hands on her hips in her red eyelet dress, thrust out her chest, and beneath her sparkling Minnie Mouse ears, exclaimed, "No! Let's do it. I'm going to be brave!" After the final five-story drop, when the ride was over, she ran up to Julie and Luke, shouting at the top of her lungs, "Look, guys! I did it! Aren't I brave?"

That experience with seven-year-old Sophia led me to question how different my life might have been if you had mothered me the way I tried to mother her in that moment. I remembered how fearless I was at a very young age and how frightened you were for me to take risks. I wondered what I might have accomplished in my life, what places I would have traveled or what chances I would have taken if you hadn't tried to instill your fears in me.

I shared with Sandra that at sixty years old, I thought I had put all this baggage behind me, but how it seemed that I was making another ring around the spiral of healing our relationship. "What's interesting," I told her, "is I no longer feel resentment toward my mother. What I feel now is sadness and grief."

When she asked me what the grief was about, I shared how it was multi-layered. It was the grief of losing my anchor. It was the grief of what I missed in life because I assumed your fears or was always trying to protect you. It was the grief of who I might have been if I hadn't felt so responsible for you and your happiness since I was a little girl. It was the grief of what I might have accomplished had I not been ashamed to fully show up in the world as my true self and trust I'd be supported. But most of all, I told her, my grief was so deep because mothering you at the end of your life made me feel like I had lost my child.

I remembered when I met you at the ambulance three days before you died. You looked at me with terrified eyes, grabbed my hand, and said, *"What would I have done if you hadn't been here?"*

That was a mantra for much of your life. I spent so many years trying to take care of you by hiding things you would judge harshly or disapprove of. I gave up me in order to protect you because you didn't approve of who I was.

But the deepest grief I feel is the loss of the mother you were to me in the final years of your life—the nurturing, appreciative, and accepting person you became. There are just so many layers of sadness that I'm still sifting through.

There were also many ways in which you were a good mother. I never lacked for physical comforts, you didn't neglect me, and I never doubted your love. You never shunned me, even though you disapproved of what you always called "my lifestyle" and it was clear I wasn't the daughter you'd hoped for. You loved me, but until very recently, you didn't accept me, and that was such a painful legacy to bear.

I'm capable now of holding a more balanced view, and I have a deeper understanding of what made you who you were. You were the baby in your family, whom everyone always protected. It was a different era with different expectations of who women should and shouldn't be. You were the product of a southern, evangelical Christian culture that I was able to escape.

Mama, my lungs are clearing now, along with my vision of who we were and who we are becoming in this new relationship we share. I sense that powerful healing is occurring for us both. I am learning how to breathe again, unencumbered by the cloud of neediness and suffocation that bound us together in unhealthy ways. We have entered a new partnership. One in which you can see clearly now too. And I trust from everything you've shared with me that you genuinely want me to be free, find my wings, and fly. I know you want my peace and freedom, and I believe that now you are able to accept me exactly as I am.

As Sandra said yesterday in our session, in many ways I was your teacher when you were on this earth. Now it seems our roles have reversed, and you are becoming mine.

So, Mama, please teach me how to breathe on my own without you. Thank you providing the nurturance my soul needs as I face the truth about our past and for the grace that is enabling us to heal.

I love you and I miss you,

Donna

October 2018

As Julie and I ate breakfast at our hotel in this morning, a beautiful crested goshawk flew past the window. Since hawks are divine messengers that symbolize freedom and flight, and eagles flying overhead represent guardianship and trust, I know you were among them, despite the fact that we are 7,500 miles away from home. Buddhists believe in non-attachment, and I hope that the beautiful White Tara I plan to hang on my office wall will remind me every time I see her of your hope for me, that I can release my grief and move forward with my life.

Some Days

Some days,
the grief feels so unbearable . . .
The loss of you in my everyday life.
The loss of my country.
The loss of goodness and decency in the world.

Some days,
the losses
take my breath away.
Struggling for air,
I bask in your love
to open my airways
and remind me . . .

That nothing is impossible.
That resurrection can happen.
That we are not doomed to fail.

Some days,
my faith in humanity
is shattered.
Bombs sent to terrorize,
politicize . . .

To make people cower.
To try and convince us
that hatred is more powerful
than love.

The leader
of the free world
dog-whistles,
"Conspiracy!"
"These 'bombs' are ruining our momentum."
Inciting violence at his rallies.
Gaslighting, then decrying,
"There's terrible hatred in our country.
And something must be done."

Some days,
I awaken
to newsfeed
of holy ground shattered.
Of innocent lives
annihilated by bullets of madmen
in churches, schools, and synagogues.
Historically safe places,
where women and children
are being slaughtered,
while seeking to learn or pray.

Some days,
the grief seems insurmountable
without you.
Despite the darkness
all around me,
I'd discovered a place of refuge
in your warm embrace.
Your love,

in your last days,
an antidote to fear.

Holding your hand,
a reminder
you would keep me safe,
until my time came
to do the same for you.

Some days,
the grief feels so unbearable,
I cannot breathe.
But I feel your love
surrounding me,
infusing me,
encouraging me . . .

To not give up.
To fight against injustice.
To focus on goodness.
To cultivate compassion.
To do my best
on my worst day,
to seek
to embody
your love.

White Tara

Hi Mama,

I'm writing from Kathmandu, Nepal. We're here on a Seva Foundation donor trip to observe the work their teams are doing to restore eyesight in this country. As Julie and I ate breakfast in our hotel this morning, a beautiful crested goshawk flew past the window. It made me smile as I thought of your spirit following us all the way around the globe, 7,500 miles from home.

I've been struggling so much the past few weeks with the anger I'm feeling about what's happening in our country. The politics are more toxic than I've experienced in my lifetime. I was happy to leave the US for three weeks and leave the news behind.

I'm trying to take the high road and focus on being loving and kind as you've asked me to do, but sometimes it feels impossible. I can't believe this is my country anymore. I'm happy you aren't here to witness what's happening to the Mexican and Central American children who are being ripped from the arms of their parents at our southern border by the US government. I know it would break your heart.

The other day before we left for our trip, as Julie and I walked the dogs at the park down the hill from our house, we had an encounter of the same kind of hatred in our own backyard.

There was a man on the trail who had two German shepherds off leash who started charging toward our dogs. When we asked him to leash them, he refused, so we took a different path, only to pass him again at the end of our walk.

We crossed the street to avoid him, but he refused to move. I asked why he was being such a jerk, and he screamed out the words "cunts" and "bull dykes" because he feels he has the right to do that since he's been emboldened by the president to say whatever hateful words he chooses. The saddest part for me is how Trump is now the de facto leader of the Christian right. He and his ilk are the antithesis of how the Jesus that you raised me to follow would treat others.

Given everything that's happening at home, it's been nice to be in a Buddhist country for a few weeks where people are truly kind. We took the Seva group to the ancient city of Bhaktapur yesterday, and while we were there we met a thangka artist, Mr. Chitraker. I wanted to buy a thangka of White Tara, who represents the Divine Mother. We spent an hour with this lovely man in his shop and he made us tea. I told him about losing you in February and how difficult it had been for me to let you go.

He found the perfect thangka he had painted, then he offered a beautiful prayer for healing grief in Nepali and wrote the prayer on the back of the piece I bought. Buddhists believe in non-attachment, and I hope that the beautiful White Tara I plan to hang on my office wall will remind me every time I see her of your hope for me, that I can learn to release my grief and move forward with my life.

This afternoon, we arrived in the city of Pokhara at the foot of the Himalayas, where we will end our trip. After we checked in to our hotel, we stepped out onto the balcony. I was overwhelmed by the majesty of the mighty Machapuchare and Annapura II mountain peaks cresting at the top of the evening sky. The view was only outdone by the majesty of the flock of hawk-eagles circling the trees from our front door. There must have been at least fifty.

Since hawks are divine messengers that symbolize freedom and flight, and eagles flying overhead represent guardianship and trust, I know you were among them, despite the fact that we are 7,500 miles away from home.

I love you and I miss you,

Donna

November 2018

I'm so thankful you aren't here to endure the wildfires and the politics of hatred igniting everywhere around us, each growing more brutal every day. As much as I've dreaded this first Thanksgiving and my first birthday without you, I'm incredibly grateful for the gift of the precious stuffed black bear you gave me, for clean air to breathe, for generous friends, and for the billowy white clouds in the heavenly sky from which you orchestrate your magic. On this sunny, warm Thanksgiving Day, I'm grateful that even though you can't sit at the table with us for dinner this year, your spirit is always near.

Nine Months

This labor of grief
is harrowing,
consumptive,
demanding . . .
Never fully letting go.

Nine months ago,
I said goodbye
to the woman
who created me,
and carried me safe
in the warmth
of your womb.

I bid farewell
to the mother
who gifted me
with the breath of life,
who fashioned
and shaped me,
into the woman
I am today.

Our labors,
though different,
now bind us
with a seamless cord
that tethers us . . .

Heart to Heart,
Soul to Soul,
Mind to Mind.

Your work,
to render me useful,
now completed.
My work,
to let you go.

The gestation
of love
comes full circle.
A spiral in time
into infinity.
An imprint
that can never
be erased.

This labor of grief
shatters,
reorders,
reconstructs,
until it is freed
to transform.

Last Chance

The world is on fire.

The air,
thick with toxic fumes,
makes it difficult to breathe.
The orange sun,
shrouded in a hazy gauze
of cyanide and PCBs.
The news rolls in,
body counts rising each day.

The world is on fire.

A horse finds shelter,
shivering on the cover
of a swimming pool.
A man and his dog,
stuck in a creek
awaiting rescue.

The world is on fire.

A president tweets,
"Sweep your forest floors!"
Six thousand troops
sent to the Texas border
for a ratings stunt,
while thousands
have no place to sleep.

The world is on fire.

Kali rages.
We are on the brink.
The forces of greed and evil
threaten to break our spirits.
Mother Earth weeps.

The world is on fire.

But the phoenix is rising.
Story after story
of first responders
carrying elders, pets,
and prized possessions
through blazing infernos.
Neighbor helping neighbor,
aid rushing in.

The world is on fire.

No more time
to be silent
or diverted,
to waste time
on hatred and division,
lose hope,
or submit to despair.

The world is on fire.

We are the ones that can save her.
Love is our only chance.

Mama Bear

Hi Mama,

Just when I thought I was finally out of the woods with my lungs, I'm back on the nebulizer again. While we were in Nepal, the air was so polluted I picked up a sinus infection, which morphed into bronchitis after we got home. With the wildfires raging here in Northern California, I can't seem to catch a break. If you were here now looking at the choking, orange skies all around us, I know just what you'd say. *"Girls, I think we're in the end times now. Maybe Jesus is on his way."*

Mama, I'm so thankful you aren't here to endure the wildfires and the politics of hatred igniting everywhere around us, each growing more brutal every day. A few weeks ago on my way to work you told me, *"Honey, in times like these you have to trust that love is coming back in style and have faith that soon it will be popular again."* Mama, you knew a lot about fashion trends when you were here, and since you're more tuned in to the bigger picture than I am, I surely hope you're right.

The past week I've been so desperate for some clean air to breathe that Julie and I decided to leave town for a while to escape this toxic air. I posted our plan on Facebook, and our friends Winston and Carol offered us their beach house near Pismo Beach to retreat for a few days. So yesterday we packed our bags and headed down the coast.

On our way to the beach last night, we stopped to pick up dinner at the Black Bear Diner in Gilroy. I was shopping for Christmas gifts for Sophia and Luke while we waited for our takeout. When I picked up a stuffed black bear, I heard your voice whispering in my ear, *"Honey, your birthday is right around the corner. Why don't you use some of the money I left you and buy that bear as a birthday gift from me. Whenever you miss me and you need a hug, just hold it tight and imagine that bear is me."*

Since I've become more compliant about following your instructions since your departure, with tears in my eyes, I shared your message with Julie. She smiled at me, took the bear from my arms, walked up to the register, and bought it. "Mama Bear" now has a new home in these almost sixty-one-year-old arms.

Mama, as much as I've dreaded this first Thanksgiving and my first birthday without you, I'm incredibly grateful for the gift of the precious stuffed black bear you gave me, for clean air to breathe, for generous friends, and for the billowy white clouds in the heavenly sky from which you orchestrate your magic. On this sunny, warm Thanksgiving Day, I'm grateful that even though you can't sit at the table with us for dinner this year, your spirit is always near.

I love you and I miss you,

Donna

Gratitude

This is the start
of a series of firsts,
this holiday season
without you.

Sixty years
of family celebrations
I watched you
in your element . . .
Brining.
Stuffing.
Basting.
Showing me
what it takes
to make things tender.

Three years ago,
we locked the door
to your house
one final time
and moved you west
on a blustery Thanksgiving Day.

Courageously,
you said goodbye
to the only home
you'd ever known,
and gave me the keys
to your heart.

Traveling through
the Dallas airport,
horrified,
I remembered
I'd checked your
diamond jewelry
in my suitcase.
The rest of the flight
I questioned
how I'd ever be able
to care for you,
if I was so neglectful.

The past two years,
surrounded
by your newfound friends,
you were so proud
to introduce me
at your community's
Thanksgiving dinner.

Your mind
no longer able
to navigate a recipe,
you didn't want us
to worry about cooking.
You fretted
that we worked too much,
and never found time to rest.

This evening,
you will not be
sitting at our table,
but you will be
resting gently
in the fissures
of a tender,
grateful heart.

Two years ago,
on my birthday
you took the bus to Macy's
because you wanted
to be certain
I had a present.

You couldn't remember
what size I wore,
so you bought a gift card
before you got lost,
and the driver
had to come inside
and find you.
You'd forgotten
how to use your phone
and call for help.

When you shared with me
what happened,
I told you
not to take the bus again
because it wasn't safe,
and I would take you
wherever you
needed to go.

I was touched
by your determination
to buy me a present
because you loved me so much,
and didn't want
to disappoint me.

I've never received a gift
more meaningful
than that plastic card
you worked so hard
to give me.

So today
I'll get through Thanksgiving,
and next week,
my birthday,
without you.

Then I'll have three weeks
to build my strength again
until Christmas,
when I'll muster
my courage again.

And at those times
when I miss you most,
I'll wrap myself
in the precious gifts
of the sweet memories
you gave me.

December 2018

"Cut out these words, sweetie, and paste them on the front cover of your birthday card. Make sure and glue the word 'darling' right under the letters that spell 'Happy Birthday.' The words 'Love Your Life' need to go on the bottom of the front cover of the card, because someday soon, I promise, you're going to feel that way again."

Birthday Card

Hi Mama,

I just returned from my parental loss bereavement group at Hospice by the Bay. I've been struggling again with depression. After I talked to the bereavement counselor, I understand what I'm feeling is situational depression, which often follows loss. It feels the same as clinical depression, which I haven't experienced for many years, so I'm happy to learn that these dark clouds hovering over me should dissipate with time.

Tonight, we had a special holiday event at hospice, and we worked with art supplies. I got clear instructions from you to make myself a birthday card, even though my birthday was last week. As I cut and pasted pictures from old magazines, I heard your sweet voice guiding every move . . .

"Cut out these words, sweetie, and paste them on the front cover. Now take that scene of the plains and the trees with the rainbow and cut it into the shape of a heart. When you get home, take the picture we took right after I moved to California of the two of us in front of the little Christmas tree in my apartment and glue it on the bottom of the heart. Now take that small pink crystal heart and paste it on the top right corner. Make sure and glue the word 'darling' right under the letters that spell 'Happy Birthday.'

"The words 'Love your life,'" you directed, *"need to go on the bottom of the front cover, because someday soon, I promise, you're going to feel that way again."*

Then you said I should cut out the life instructions I found in a magazine and glue them on the inside of the left front cover:

. . . start doing things you love . . . have an open heart . . . make a difference . . . no beauty shines brighter than that of a good heart . . . life doesn't have to be perfect to be wonderful . . . you are capable of becoming more than you realize . . . throw kindness around like confetti . . . live, create, tell the story . . . be your beautiful self . . . do more than exist . . . choose to see the good . . . you are enough . . . and, of course . . . don't forget to fly . . .

Then you pointed me to a blue butterfly and some radiant 3D stars, and the card was almost complete. When I came home tonight, you reminded me to go through the old birthday cards you'd written me over the years and read them all again. When my hands landed on a particular message, you instructed, *"Sweetie, cut this out and put it on the inside of your card."* Written in your handwriting when you could still see were the words you wrote ten years ago:

"What joy you have brought to me and how grateful I am for your love. May your birthday be filled with fun, with laughter, and a little extra rest worked in there somewhere. Do know how much I love you and wish I could be there and share this day with you. I love you more than I could ever express and thank you for your help. Your Mama."

Thank you, Mama, for helping me create the perfect birthday card.

I'm going to keep it on my desk so I will always have a reminder of how much you loved me then and still love me now, Divine Mother of my heart.

I love you and I miss you,

Donna

Learning to Dance

Grief reshapes
the contours
of an aching heart.
Softly and subtly
the hardest losses
remake us,
open us
to a presence so deep
that we are transformed—
rendered kinder,
more trusting,
more whole.

The ego's will,
destabilized,
forged in the fires
of longing.
Transformed
into a guiding hand,
rather than a master
seeking to control.

Grief upends
normality,
recalibrates meaning,
restores order,
redefines
what's most important.

Grief cracks the heart
wide open.
Revealing fissures
once shut tight,
enabling vulnerabilities
once deemed weaknesses
to sparkle
and transcend
the glistening veil
of pure,
eternal love.

Grief reshapes,
if we allow its alchemy
to touch us.
Its grace,
to remake us.
Its call,
to remind us
the reason
we took birth
is to learn
how to dance
with love.

Watching the Herring Spawn

I sit on my perch
at the top of the hill
watching the herring spawn.

Remembering the last morning
we spent,
arm in arm,
in our fuzzy pink robes
with teacups in hand,
eleven months ago.

I loved sharing those moments with you.
Watching your eyes light up in wonder
at nature's mysteries,
water shimmering like stars
beneath our feet.
You'd never seen so many seagulls in one place,
you said,
having grown up on the plains.

You were beginning to grow feeble.
Your mind, more brittle.
But your heart
opened wider
to me,
to the world,
to the loving kindness
you'd become.

The seabirds,
marking a new year . . .

The first year
I'll be on my own
without your hand to hold,
or the sound of your laughter
to comfort me
on difficult days.

The first year
I won't be taking care of you,
assuring you of your safety,
and promising
to be your brain
as your memory faded away.

When I said goodbye to you
forty-six weeks ago,
I didn't think
I could love you more
than I did then,
but I do.

I never thought
that you'd turn out to be

the one
guiding me now,
but you are.

I never imagined
the sorrow
that came with your loss
could open my heart
as it has.

I never knew
the gifts of grief
could remake
and transform me
with love's deepest knowing.

As I watch the herring spawn,
I bask in wonder
of the mystery
of our new bond,
of who I will grow into
untethered to you,
but ever grateful
for the never-ending wisdom
of your ever-present love.

January 2019

Just when I thought I was ready to reenter the world again, fate had other plans. It seems my only course of action now is to learn to surrender and rest. Please help me navigate this new twist of fate. Shower me with patience and strength to quickly recover from my accident. And thank you for always being there to catch me when I fall.

Twist of Fate

Hi Mama,

I survived the holidays without you, even though I was convinced on Christmas Day that I'd be spending them with you. Ron and I decided it would be too painful to have our traditional Christmas celebration at our house this year, so we decided to meet in Colorado and go skiing with the kids. We remembered how much it helped to do something different than our normal celebration when the three of us took that skiing trip the Christmas after Daddy died forty years ago.

Julie, Sophia, and I went sledding the day before Christmas. It was wonderful to laugh and play with her again since we hadn't seen the children since last summer. There's nothing like the antics of a seven-year-old to lift your spirits.

I imagined how horrified you'd be when Sophia flew out of the hot tub in her bathing suit after we returned to the cabin. In bare feet, she jumped into the snow, lay down, and with great delight, spent the next few minutes making snow angels until the ground was covered in her image. *"Get that child out of the snow right now and wrap her up!"* I could hear you yelling from the ethers. *"She'll catch her death of cold."*

We opened our gifts early Christmas morning, then grabbed our gear and headed for the slopes. Ron, Kenji, and the kids took skiing lessons, and Julie and I rented skis and headed up the lift. It had been five years since we'd been skiing, but muscle memory quickly returned.

After several runs down the easy slopes, we grew more self-assured, graduating to the intermediate ones. On the last run of the day, as I barreled down the hill, ironically named "Ghost Rider," I separated from Julie halfway down the mountain as she turned right and I veered left. It was a gorgeous, sunny, springlike day as I congratulated myself for turning in a perfect parallel. *Wow*, I thought, *I remember now! This is what joy feels like*—a foreign feeling these past eleven months.

Then bam! The next thing I knew my ski caught an edge, and my body started spinning, skis flipping over my head. The last thing I remember was my head slamming into the hard, icy ground, until I opened my eyes and was greeted by fluffy white clouds and the warm sun beating down on my face. My first conscious thought was, *Oh my God, I must have died! Now I get to spend Christmas with Mama in heaven!*

Then I felt someone shaking my shoulder trying to rouse me, as droplets of water rained down on my face. I looked up to see Julie sobbing, trying to catch her breath. "Honey, wake up. Are you okay?" she anxiously implored. "You've been out stone cold for the last few minutes. I was afraid that you were dead."

Several strangers stood around us forming a human shield so that no one would hit me while racing down the hill. A few minutes later, the ski patrol arrived, shined a light in my eyes, and asked me a bunch of questions I can't remember. Then they gathered me up, put my neck in a brace, and strapped me on a sled.

Later that night at the hospital, the doctor told me I'd sustained a serious concussion. "If you hadn't been wearing a helmet," he said, "you might not be here now to tell the tale." Since we came home from Colorado two weeks ago, I've spent most of the time sequestered in our bedroom with the shades drawn. I saw the neurologist a few days ago and was told I'd sustained some damage to my brain that I'll be working with a physical therapist to try and heal.

Mama, just when I thought I was ready to reenter the world again, it seems fate had other plans. My gait is still unsteady and my balance is off, so I'm using hiking poles to walk. My eyes still aren't yet tracking in unison, so it's hard to read or write. My head still throbs and the headaches are unrelenting, so I've been taking Vicodin and am feeling very disconnected from the world. My only course of action now is to learn to surrender and rest.

I cannot even begin to express how excited I was when I thought I would see you again, but when I came to, I also realized how much Julie needed me and wanted me to stay. I've made peace with the fact that it wasn't my time to leave the planet. I may never be able to ski again, but I hope the joy I felt in those moments before my wipeout will return again one day.

Mama, please help me navigate this new twist of fate. Shower me with patience and strength to quickly recover from my accident. And thank you for always being there to catch me when I fall.

I love you and I miss you,

Donna

Listening to the Rain

The rain,
falling like tears
on a gray
winter's day . . .

Remembering you
a year ago,
standing guard
at the doorway
by the threshold,
terrified
the approaching storm
would spawn tornadoes,
or the waves
three hundred feet below
would somehow rise
and drown us.

I assured you we didn't
have tornadoes here,
that you were safe,
and these kinds of storms

were normal
at wintertime
in Northern California.

I had no idea
it would be the last time
we'd watch the rain together.

I've now traversed
all the first anniversaries
without you,
except the last one,
the day I kissed your forehead,
gave your hand to God,
and said my last goodbye.

Losing you
has been the hardest path
I've ever trodden.
Letting you go
was the thing
I always dreaded,
and hoped I could avoid,
even though it was expected—
a natural storm
in the cycle of loss
adult children
must endure.

Since you died,
I've kept one foot in heaven
and both eyes on the stars,
my broken heart ravaged
on jagged rocks,
against the windswept shore.

I've cycled through heartbreak,
denial, depression, anger . . .
and gratitude,
you didn't have to linger,
wear a diaper,
or completely lose your mind.

Thankful you were able
to leave this earth
with your dignity intact.

Since you left
eleven months ago
there have been days
I've been breathless,
unable to function from grief.
And others,
where I've watched you
swoop down
from your nest
high atop the trees,
delighting in your antics.

For all my life
I yearned for the mother
you became to me
in your last days,
as we opened our hearts
in forgiveness,
and traded
criticism for compassion,
judgment for appreciation,
and hopelessness for faith
in who we learned
that we could be together.

This bittersweet loss
of longing
for what we had
at the end of your life
is relentless,
and makes it feel unbearable
to detach
and let you go.

January rain
falls gently now
like the salt in my tears
as I savor
the gifts
you've delivered
from heaven,
and cherish the moments
we shared
in your last years
on earth.

My greatest treasure,
the chance to heal
that primal wound
I carried within
for so many years,
through the bounty of love
at the end of your life
that you gave me.

February 2019

Three days before you died, the nurse asked you if you knew where you were. You responded, "I think I'm in the coming home place." I think I'm in the coming home place too, just in a different way. I trust this difficult journey through this portal of grief will help me learn how to come home to myself. Thank you and all your messengers for guiding me and helping me find my way home.

February

The month
of your birth
and your death
has arrived.
Polar winds
tug me homeward,
as I steel myself
in preparation
for the days ahead.

Last Valentine's Day,
I held your hand
and said goodbye.
You waited
another day
before you drew
your final breath,
not wanting
that day of love
marked by sadness
for those you loved
each year.

The hours you lay dying
were the hardest
I've ever encountered.
When your breathing ceased,
we washed your
worn-out body
whose petite,
tender arms
had embraced
me so often,
whose heart
had touched
so many lives.

We made the journey
to your final resting place,
on your beloved plains of Texas.
I did my best to honor you.
My words, inept,
to share my gratitude
for giving me life,
for doing your best
to craft me
into a woman
you could leave behind,
trusting I would try my best
to live the love you taught me.

Our family rallied
around me.
Cousins became sisters,
strangers became friends.
The garden
of companions
you planted and tended

over the years,
offered their final farewells.

I carried a spray of flowers
from your burial plot
through the howling winds
to your mother's grave,
so grateful
you were finally reunited.

A year has passed . . .

I am no longer
the same person
I was then.
My heart is wider.
My love is deeper.
My capacity
to walk both worlds
has expanded.
Yet I still pray
that my ability
to experience joy
will someday soon
return.

Deep grief
has been the potter
that has taken the shards
of my greatest loss,
and mercifully reformed them
into a vessel of love
I hope will make you proud.

Valentine's Day

On Valentine's Day
a year ago,
we sat vigil . . .

Waiting for you
to make your final journey
Home.

I laid a card on your heart,
held your soft, swollen hand,
and recited its words,
hoping that you
could still hear them.

The nurses came
and took your roses away,
my final gift to you.

On Valentine's Day
a year ago,
we sat vigil.

Today, I'm wrapped
in the red velour hoodie
I gave you
as a token of my love.
Like a child's garment
two sizes too small,
your scent
still lingering in the fibers,
as I imagine
your warm embrace.

On Valentine's Day
a year ago,
we sat vigil.

This morning,
on my drive to work
you greeted me.
Comforted by your loving words,
you shared
how Valentine's Day in heaven
was like Christmas here on earth . . .
"Love's crowning glory,"
you said,
"a feast of abiding love."

You encouraged me
to spend the anniversary
of your Homecoming
not in mourning,
but in celebration
of your arrival
to your eternal Home.

You said the greatest gift
that I could give you

was finding joy again.
That I could miss you,
but should no longer mourn you,
as you were always
by my side.

You thanked me
for being such a blessing
in your final years,
for taking care of you,
and for helping you leave this world,
just as you had helped me in.

You said we should spend
the anniversary
of your Homecoming
at the de Young Museum,
gazing at the water lilies
we'd seen together
at the Kimbell,
many years before.

You told me since
you no longer had a body,
you now loved
to gaze at the world
through my eyes,
to see the things
that in your blindness,
you were unable
to discern.

Being in a room full of beauty,
you whispered,
would be a fitting way
to mark your journey
Home.

You told me when I missed you
to remember
the sound of your laughter.
You encouraged me
to gird myself
in the strength of your love,
to know the angels
always travel with me,
and to put my trust
in God.

A year ago
on Valentine's Day,
we sat vigil.

Tomorrow,
we mark your heavenly birthday
with grateful hearts,
for the promise
and the blessing
of your ever-present love.

Your Birthday

Today is your birthday.
My heart,
heavy with grief,
and light with joy,
for you are finally free.
I envision you celebrating
with the people you love.
I see your mother
and my father
tenderly embrace you,
so grateful you are Home.

Remembering your instructions
not to mourn
for you,
like a little child
so proud of her accomplishments,
you ask me to imagine
all that you can do now.

I see you run,
then dance, and fly.
Your "bone on bone" knee,

no longer a deterrent.
Your Swiss cheese brain,
now whole,
and ever knowing.

Remembering your last ten birthdays
since your husband died,
I never wanted you to be alone,
or feel lonely.
Each year,
I felt so grateful
to share another celebration,
another year of life
with you.

This year,
I commemorate
the gift you are now,
as I watch you
tenderly reweave
the jagged,
frayed threads
of my heart.

Since you left,
you've never stopped
reminding me
to get more rest,
to rely on God's grace for comfort,
to hold the teddy bear you gave me
when I miss you,
and to remember
I'm never alone.

Today, I bought you flowers
and placed them on the altar

by your picture.
As I gaze into your eyes,
I see the love
you've always felt for me.
The flicker of the candle
dancing on your gentle face
warms my aching heart.

I'm so grateful
that we took the risk
to fan its flame,
and found the courage
to allow it
to light the way
to unconditional love.

This birthday,
your gift to me,
your presence.
My gift to you,
a bouquet of devotion
bursting through the soil
of a full and grateful heart.

Blue Jay

Hi Mama,

Today would have been your eighty-ninth birthday. Since it wasn't possible to bring flowers to your grave in Texas, I've been sitting on the terrace on your garden bench listening to the surf as it sweeps on the shore between rainstorms.

As I gazed at the angel statue I bought as a memorial for you last year on my first Mother's Day without you, memories from a year ago flooded my heart . . . those three awful days when you were in the hospital and we sat vigil as you bled to death . . . the moment you opened your eyes to say goodbye as you drew your last breath after two days of being unconscious . . . standing by your gravesite as the frigid winter winds ravaged the flowers on your grave and nearly blew us over . . . my acknowledgment as we left to catch the plane back to California that the final chapter of my life in Texas had ended, knowing I had no choice but to leave you in the frozen ground, never to see you again . . .

The tears flowed as I remembered your birthdays that we celebrated . . . your 65th and surprise 70th we threw for you at Lake Kiowa when Daddy Jack was still alive . . . your 80th at First Baptist Church in Gainesville when you asked Ron and me not to wear our wedding rings so none of your friends would discover your children were gay . . .

After all the festivities ended that night, I cornered you in your kitchen. "You've broken my heart," I sobbed, my voice cracking as I wept. That was the most honest conversation we'd had until that point. It was also the day we committed to healing our relationship after many years of fits and starts.

In some ways, Mama, it feels like you left us yesterday. In others, it feels like an eternity since you've been gone. I'm so grateful I captured all the videos and phone messages of you sharing how much you loved and appreciated Julie and me in the months before you died. I wish I'd asked you how you felt about dying before you could no longer speak, but everything happened so quickly.

As I sat on your bench this morning reflecting on this past year without you, a blue jay flew down from the olive tree and lit on the rim of the birdbath four feet away. Some Native peoples believe that blue jays are messengers from heaven that have the power to connect us to our ancestors, so I knew you'd sent her as a totem to comfort me today.

As I was relishing the beauty of her azure-blue head and the white-and-indigo-blue speckled patterns in her feathers, she dove her beak into the birdbath to get a drink of water. As she raised her head and looked up at me, I heard your sweet voice whisper, *"Honey, I am right here with you, and I am sorry you're still sad. I want you to be happy again, to reclaim your joy, and relish every moment of your life. And I want you to know that I'm exactly where I am supposed to be on my birthday this year, and I am finally free. And freedom from pain is also what I want for you."*

Then you continued, *"Honey, keep resting, and continue to heal your heart and your head. It's okay if this journey takes a while longer before you emerge on the other side. You can't rush through this. Just remember, sweetheart, like the good book says, for everything there is a season. This is your season of darkness and rain. But spring will come soon, I promise. The crocus will bloom. The fledging hawks will leave their nests and fly. And the sun will break free from the clouds and light your way again. But no matter which season you're experiencing in your life, always know I'll be there with you, loving you with all my heart."*

Mama, thank you for the messenger you sent to greet me today and for your sweet message of encouragement and love. Thank you for helping my head and heart begin to mend, even though it's taking much longer than I'd planned. Some days are harder than others, but I know I am never alone. What I am learning now is that the smallest gesture of kindness may be the one thing that can turn despair into hope, and sadness into gratitude. How thankful I am to have a divine mother who continues to seed such powerful, healing wisdom in my heart.

Three days before you died when I met you at the hospital, the nurse asked you if you knew where you were. You responded, *"I think I'm in the coming home place."*

Mama, I think I'm in the coming home place too, just in a different way. I trust this difficult journey through this portal of grief will help me come home to myself. So happy birthday, Mama. Thank you and all your messengers for guiding me and for helping me find my way home.

I love you and I miss you,

Donna

April 2019

I now see that it took losing you, followed by my head injury, to dismantle me at my core and help me remember what's most important. Through the wisdom you've shared in our many conversations, you've enabled me to find a deeper connection to my own divinity. I'm beginning to feel rays of hope, glimmers of possibility, and a deep sense of gratitude for everything I'm learning on this journey, despite how challenging it's been.

The Long, Dark Winter

This long, dark year of winter is ending,
just as you promised it would.

The light through the trees
is different now.
It's brighter,
more hopeful,
less gray.
The air I breathe
is less oppressive.
Crisp and clean,
it welcomes me
back to life
and living.

Blossoms of spring
burst forth
from your pink geraniums
potted on our terrace,
bringing color
to the empty bench
where you once sat.

The rains are waning,
still incomplete,
but a pungent
air of hope
now fills the air,
affirming progress.

Feeling inspired
to write again,
to tell our story.
To share how the bonds
of great love
are endless,
and can make you better,
not bitter,
if you trust
love never ends.

This long, dark year of winter
has transformed me.
I am quieter,
less frenzied,
more present in each moment,
less driven by my ego,
more settled in my heart.

My grief has been the chrysalis—
the web of love
you knitted
to hold me
and protect me,
as I've struggled
to make meaning
of your passage,
and craft a life
without you here.

You asked me
to focus on your presence,
and never lose faith
that I was tended
in your care.

Now I know
that you will never
leave me.
Your soft embrace
still cradles me
in this metamorphosis
of becoming
someone different.
Stretching my wings
and trusting,
someday soon
I'll fly.

Beauty and Loss

After you died,
you told me my work now
was to learn to build a bridge
between heaven and earth.
To do my best
to bring comfort and love
to a hurting world.
To trade
in the currency
of kindness,
and offer my heart
to those
who needed care.

I once believed
creating heaven on earth
meant cultivating
a garden of joy.
Yet now I know
its roots go much deeper.
Its veins, more complex.
Its strength, more fragile.

In the compost of loss,
tendrils are formed
through the dark night of death.
And true beauty
cannot blossom
without the nutrients
of patience, faith, and hope.

Now I see
the integration
of beauty and loss
is possible,
and a necessary stage
of resurrection
and ascension
into a rose,
once battered and bruised
by the elements of grief.

Now capable
of blooming fully—
a living testament
to the power
of your ever-present love.

Tree of Life

Hi Mama,

Spring has arrived! And just as you promised, the pain in my head and in my heart is beginning to ease. I've been getting out most days with my hiking poles and walking a mile or two, working to regain my balance so I'm ready for my trip to England in a few weeks. After my accident, I was afraid I wouldn't be able to make the journey, but physical therapy has been very helpful, and I'm making great progress each day.

One way I've been occupying my time as I've been recovering from my concussion is taking an online class with Dr. Andrew Harvey on the dark night of the soul. In our first session, he said this challenging time we're experiencing in the world is a collective dark night of the soul. He believes we're being called to integrate the spiritual and human aspects of our being, so we can transform into the divine humans we are intended to become.

As I've listened to these classes, I've realized how much time and energy I've focused on the material world over the last ten years. In my pursuit of achieving my goals and acquiring more things, I've spent precious little time tending to my spirit. As a result, in some ways, it feels like my body has grown disconnected from my spirit.

I see now that it took losing you, followed by my head injury, to dismantle me at my core and help me to remember what's most important. And everything that's happened was necessary to enable me to begin to integrate into that divine human being I've been longing to become for many years.

One of the practices Andrew invited us to do was to repeat the name of the divine each day. What I realized as I've been experimenting with that practice is how you've become my bridge to the divine since your death. Through the wisdom you've shared in our many conversations, you've enabled me to find a deeper connection to my own divinity and to bring greater light into the world. As a result, I'm beginning to feel rays of hope, glimmers of possibility, and a deep sense of gratitude for everything I'm learning on this journey, despite how challenging it's been.

I'm reminded of your advice three weeks ago as I drove home from the doctor's office. I passed a large panel truck with a graphic of a large green oak tree bearing many branches. Inscribed underneath the tree were the words "Tree of Life." I heard your voice whisper, *"Honey, look at that oak tree on the side of that truck. That's what I'm here to teach you. Your work now is to be an emissary of love and light. Grace will sustain you though every challenge you face in your life if you allow it space to enter. Just keep your heart open, seek to love deeply, and keep giving whatever you can, whenever you can, wherever you can. Focus on detaching from your ego so that more light can shine through. Allow your acorn to grow into a shelter of solace for those in need of care."*

A week after that, we took Luke and Sophia to Monterey for their spring break, and we stopped at Cannery Row for ice cream. I pointed to the shop across the street and told Sophia I was sad because the last time I'd been there was when I took Nana there to buy her a T-shirt when she was a baby. Your wise granddaughter took my hand, looked me in the eyes, and said, "Aunt Donna, instead of thinking about what happened then, why don't you think about how much fun we're having now, and then you won't be so sad?"

It was another lesson from your granddaughter, my youngest teacher, to focus on finding joy in the present moment, rather than holding so tightly to the past. I'm so blessed by the innocent words of a child on this earth and the wise words of my mama, my divine channel, from heaven.

What I'm realizing, through this journey of grief and through being forced to move slowly as I've worked to heal my head injury, is that I no longer want my life to be focused on driving to make things happen through sheer force of will. What I choose now is to trust that whatever I need will emerge in divine timing. All I need to do is to hold that faith and remain open to the possibilities around me, so that I'm able to receive what's coming next.

The other day, my friend Noreen said she sensed that when I slammed my head into that mountain, even though I had the chance to go and be with you, I chose to stay here because my soul knew my work here wasn't finished.

And now, as I watch the tulips and azaleas bloom on our dog walks in the morning and the skies clear from winter's rains, I sense that I'm emerging from the dark night of the soul I entered when I saw that portal as I was falling to sleep three months before you died. I knew then, but didn't yet want to admit, that something fundamentally needed to change. What has transformed is my understanding of life's fragility and my ability to feel and observe the vast storehouse of beauty around me.

What's clear now is that it's impossible to know beauty without loss or to experience loss without beauty. And joy emerges when I'm fully present to beauty. Through beauty, I see possibility. Through beauty, I feel hope. I'm learning there's even beauty in the dung heaps of life when I stop long enough to see it. Mama, it's the integration of your loss with the gifts of everything I've gained through your teachings and your steadfast love that's enabling me to experience true beauty.

There's a lot about my life that's different now. I'm living at a much less frenzied pace. I'm settling into a softer, quieter life, the kind you always wanted me to have. I'm learning how to rest in the divine, ground myself in the beloved, be grateful for the present moment, and thankful for each day that I have left. There's so much beauty everywhere around me. Thank you for helping me open my heart to receive it.

Mama, I'm so grateful for everything you're teaching me, for your divine presence, for the power of your words to heal and transform, and most of all, for the promise of your eternal love. I'm thankful for my head injury because it's shifted my priorities. Even though I thought I was ready to reenter the world earlier this year, divine timing had other plans. With your help, I'm patiently awaiting what will emerge as I am transformed into a divine human being, because that is what I yearn to be and that is who I am.

I love you and I miss you,

Donna

May 2019

"The time for mourning is now over. Today at the Chalice Well, you passed through the portal of grief, and now you've emerged on the other side. So live now, sweetheart. Truly live. Thrive, grow, and bring your gifts to the world. Don't hold back. It's time for you to manifest your dreams, and I am here to help you learn to create heaven on earth. This is your calling."

On the Train
to Edinburgh

The green fields
of my ancestors
entreat my soul
to listen
to their voices
of windswept wisdom,
and embrace
these lands
from which I came.

A holy gray sky
illuminates,
calling me
to journey deeper.
Unearthing memories
of lives once lived
on this mystical path,
in this place
I once called home.

Those dear to my heart
accompany me.
My father, my mother,
my grandmothers,
the spirits
of my clan.
They circle
and enfold me.
No longer
an outlander
on this sodden earth.
At last,
returning home.

Their shimmering rays
of love transform,
tears of joy
descend.

Grief lifts
its dark,
heavy veil
from the chain of light
that illuminates
and binds.

Woven strong,
from generation
to generation.
Life to life.
Era to era.

The wings
of the Great Beloved
carry us all

across the ocean
of distance, place, and time.
Its grace . . .
Eternal.
Still.

Finding My Way Home

Restormel Manor
Cornwall, England

Flitting through the trees
in your majestic glory,
I call your name . . .

Five thousand miles from home,
fifteen months since you departed,
you still answer.

Your bright, light wings
circling above
in ever-closer concentric circles.
Weaving your unceasing love,
warp and weft,
within my heart and being.

Months ago I asked you
if you sent the hawk,
or if the hawk was what you became?
"Whatever you need,"
you told me.

Thank you for bringing
this wondrous creature
so close to me.

For continuing
to travel with me.

For always staying near.

For teaching me
how to love
beyond boundaries.

But most of all,
for helping me
find my way home.

St. Michael's Mount

Divine Beloved,
penetrate my heart
with your sword of truth.
Re-craft me as a chalice—
a vessel
capable
of washing the world
in your love.

Grant me clarity
to speak your truth
to those in need of healing.

Hold me, always near
to the angels
in your ever-widening circle
of knowing.

Embrace me
until I can no longer breathe
my own breath,
now only able

to exhale
the mist
of deep compassion.

Enfold me in grace
in the palm of your hand.
Reconstruct my thoughts
to think first of you,
without hesitation,
before moving my feet
to action.

Transmute my ego
through the alchemy
of blessed grace,
and turn this
rusting metal armor
into a tapestry of gold.

Touch me
with your sovereignty.
Help me
release my will,
and unify my intentions
with ceaseless joy
for all creation.

Great Ocean of Light,
I surrender
my body to you
on this holy hill,
as I drown in the sea
of your love.

Mother Mary

Hi Mama,

I've just returned from three weeks in Scotland and England. Our Avalon journey was one of the most magical and transformational experiences of my life. I felt your spirit with me from the second I arrived and boarded the train to Edinburgh for my solo adventure. And you were with me when I met my traveling companions in London as we wound our way for the next two weeks from Ston Easton, Somerset, to Stonehenge, to Avebury, to Cornwall, and finally, to Glastonbury. Before I left, you told me in one of our chats how much you were looking forward to seeing the world though my eyes. I hope you enjoyed our adventure!

Thank you, Mama, for giving me the nudge to take this trip and for making it possible for me to go. I'm so grateful I heeded the call. I returned with not only a wonderful new community of friends, but a family of kindred spirits who will forever be etched in my heart. Each day was filled with miracles and healing.

I will never forget your words as I sat on the park bench listening to the sweet melodies of the River Fowey outside our beautiful lodgings at Restormel Manor in Cornwall ten days ago. We'd just returned from visiting the Chalice Well in

Glastonbury, and I was trying to process everything I'd experienced. Your sweet voice lilted through the birdsong, and I remember your words.

"*Honey,*" you said, "*the time for mourning is now over. Today at the Chalice Well, you passed through the portal of grief and have emerged on the other side. That was the consecration you received this morning. Remember when your friend Pauline offered you a blessing and she told you that you would learn to dance with me in new ways? Not in mourning, but in the knowing I am always there for you. Her words were clear and true.*"

You continued, "*So live now, sweetheart. Truly live. Thrive, grow, and bring your gifts to the world. Don't hold back. No more fear. That's what I want for you.*"

"*You are living in a circle of grace,*" you shared, "*just like that beautiful creature that's flying overhead.*" I looked up and saw the magnificent goshawk circling above me, and I knew it was you who'd sent her.

"*It's time for you to manifest your dreams, and I am here to help you. I am holding your hand and guiding you. You will be provided for, protected, and cared for all the days of your life, so don't be afraid anymore. Just know that I will always be there to support you and will never leave your side. I am embedded like a golden thread that runs through your heart in this life and for eternity,*" you said with such deep clarity and love.

"*What you've been experiencing on this journey to Avalon is what I'm here to help you do, to learn to create heaven on earth. This is your calling.*"

Yesterday, when I went to your garden on our terrace to tell you how grateful I was to be experiencing joy again, I acknowledged I finally trusted everything would be okay after such a difficult fifteen months. I heard you whisper through the breeze, "*Honey, nothing brings me greater joy than seeing you happy again.*"

At that moment, a beautiful blue jay popped down from the sky and perched on the ground at my feet. She looked up and caught my eye, then quickly flew across the rocks to your angel statue on the terrace. She perched on the angel's head surveying the garden for thirty seconds, looked at me one more time, then flitted off into the trees.

You were sending me a sign to help me understand the dream I had last night. In my dream, you died a second time, and I sensed you hadn't really left us fifteen months ago. I was worried the dream meant that you were going to leave me now that I was feeling better and finally be on your way. But as I've had some time to reflect on its meaning, I realize what it portends is that I have come to a place of acceptance and peace that you're not coming back again in physical form, but your spirit will always be with me.

Mama, you told me a few weeks after you died that it would take me a year or two to heal and feel whole. I want you to know I'm almost there. You said you would always be there when I needed you, and after all the ways you've helped me these past fifteen months, I deeply trust that promise.

As I sat at the Chalice Well in Glastonbury, the site where Mary Magdalene is believed to have led Christ's followers following his crucifixion, and where Joseph of Arimathea is said to have placed a chalice with drops of Christ's blood, I reflected on the women named Mary who have graced my life. So many connections are now aligning between the Divine Mother and you, my birth mother Mary, and Mary Magdalene, and Mary the mother of Jesus. I hold each of you with reverence and gratitude for all that you're continuing to teach me.

Mama, I am grateful that on the trip to Avalon, I finally experienced heaven on earth, and for that blessing, I am deeply grateful. Thank you for being that golden thread that weaves through my heart with every breath I take.

And now, I trust the time has come for us to dance.

I love you and I miss you,

Donna

June 2019

A year and a half ago, in my last mentoring session with Jean Houston, she told me she sensed that I would write a book about divine, transcendent love. "How in the world could I ever write a book like that?" I questioned. "I know so little about that topic. It would be a fraud." You died three months later, and everything I thought I knew about the power of love and about what was possible in the afterlife was radically upended.

Remembrance

After you died,
I promised
I would share our memories,
that I would do my best
to be your voice
and share the gift
that you most valued—
the power of Kindness and Love.

The first two winters of grief,
now behind me.
The wound is deep,
but no longer
as oppressive.
The tidal rivers of tears
now run less often—
a slow and gentle rain.

Scanning through posts
from people who loved you,
and those who love me,
I sift through pages

of memories
and miracles . . .
Blessings
of how you held me,
and never left my side
in my darkest days
of grief.

I read your words,
page after page,
of ethereal transmissions.

Each one, shining light
on my passage
to do my best
as your ambassador,
to help create heaven
on earth.

My tears now
flow from gratitude
for the person you were
while you were here,
and for who you've
become since you died.

You were my guardian.
I was your caregiver.
Now you are my teacher,
showing me
how to tread this path—
both human and divine.

Each signal and sign
placed before me,

every hawk flying past,
each heart-shaped rock
that graced my feet,
bumper stickers
on cars on the freeway . . .

Each with a message,
strategically placed
to guide me.

A succession
of love songs
you've sent me,
bursting forth
into bloom
in the pictures
and words
on these pages.

After you died,
you told me
it would take
a year or two
to heal
from a loss
whose depths
I'd never known,
but whose gifts
have set me free
to open my heart,
to slow my pace,
to pray,
to rest,
and be.

May our words
be a balm
of grace
for those
who need them,
Divine Mother of my heart.

Transcendent Love

Hi Mama,

I've finally emerged from the underbelly of grief and resumed my place in the world. I still miss you more than words can express, but the pain of your loss is subsiding, and a powerful integration has occurred. I feel your presence within me now as much I once felt you around me.

A year and a half ago, in my last mentoring session with Jean Houston, she told me she sensed that I would write a book about love. I was taken aback when she made that pronouncement. She was clear the theme of the book wouldn't be about romantic love but about love that was divine and transcendent.

"How in the world could I ever write a book like that?" I questioned. "I know so little about that topic. It would be a fraud." You died three months later, and everything I thought I knew about the power of love and about what was possible in the afterlife was radically upended.

Over these past sixteen months, you've been such a powerful teacher, comforter, and way-shower to reveal the kind of love Jean spoke about. Since your death, I've observed multiple signs and symbols of your presence everywhere around me. I have listened to the wisdom of the many loving words you've whispered in my ear. And now I have a much deeper understanding of the immeasurable power of transcendent love to heal and make us whole across the dimensions of time and space, of heaven and earth, and even life and death.

When I was on the train from London to Edinburgh six weeks ago, you assured me that during that trip, my next steps would be revealed. One of the gifts I brought back from Avalon was the inspiration to write a book about our journey, because now I've experienced firsthand what transcendent love truly is. In these past few weeks as I've been writing, I feel you guiding my hands on the keyboard and whispering just the right words in my ear.

As I've pored through the posts I've posted on Facebook and the poems and letters I've written since your death, I discovered the letter I wrote at the final session of my bereavement group six months ago. I'd completely forgotten it even existed. On the outside of the envelope, I'd written, "Open June 17, 2019." The instructions the grief counselor gave us the night we wrote them was to write a letter to ourselves about where we believed we'd be on our grief journey six months later.

As I picked up a blank sheet of paper that night, your voice channeled these words through my pen.

Hello Darling,

It's your Mama. I'm writing to tell you how proud I am of you and of all the healing you've accomplished over the past year. I promised you that it would take a year or two before you would begin to feel whole again, and I see you're right on track!

Honey, what I'm most proud of is how committed you've been to keeping your heart open, despite the depths of your pain. This has continued to enable you to grow into a more loving and caring person. I've watched you rely on God's grace to get you through each day, and to use that huge storehouse of love in your heart in the way you treat and care for others.

I also want to thank you for the many ways you've honored me since my passing. I couldn't have asked for a more loving daughter when I was alive, nor a more grateful one since I've been gone. I hope you know, beyond a shadow of a doubt by now, that I am always with you. A fractal of my soul now lives in your heart, and I am here to guard and guide you now and for all eternity, as your Divine Mother.

I am grateful and proud that you've continued to use your gifts and that you will share them with others through your writing. I know they will help many on their journeys of love and loss. Your words can bring them the comfort of knowing that loss always leads back to love as long as you keep your heart open, and that losing someone you love will make you better if you don't allow it to make you bitter.

Sweetheart, I love you, I am deeply proud of you, and I promise you that I will never let go of your hand.

Your Mama

It was such a gift to find that letter today. And it's such a joy to be back at my desk writing again. I am honored to tell the story of our healing journey as we both surrendered to the mystery of grace. I'm so grateful you are my partner in this work of sharing what it is like to open yourself to experience the impact of an ever-deepening love in this world and the next.

Thank you, Mama, for continuing to shine the light above me, the light within me, and the light around me everywhere I go.

I love you and I miss you,

Donna

2020

"You are living in the midst of the great reckoning now on earth. Everyone is being called to choose a side. Will you choose love, or will you choose hatred? Will you choose hope, or will you choose fear? Every decision each one makes will collectively determine the final outcome. Never forget, my darling, that you always have a choice."

In These Quiet Days

In these quiet days,
the world stops in its tracks.
Commerce ceases.

Human touch,
replaced by technology
because it's safer,
as we wait
in silence and trepidation,
for what is yet to come.

I think of you
as we say goodbye
at a rapid clip
to aged parents,
to the weak and infirm,
to the young,
filled with hope and promise.
Robbed of breath,
they must walk on.
No time to process their losses,

before the next wave
of grief rolls in.

We say farewell
to blaring horns
in rush hour traffic.
There's space now
to hear the sounds
of snoring dogs at our feet,
grateful to finally have
our full attention.

We say hello
to cleaner air,
to fresher water,
to walks at noon
in the middle of a workday.
We stand in awe
of the majesty
of cherry blossoms blooming,
we were too busy
to notice before.

We watch the stock market plunge
with each passing day.
Our dreams for the future uncertain,
but shifting
to what matters most,
more time with the people we love.

In these quiet days
we seek to manage our anxieties,
teach our children,
work from home,
maintain social distance,
while learning to be kinder,

more patient,
more willing to sacrifice conveniences,
and open our hearts
to love.

In these quiet days
we see the best in us
in the worst of times,
through the tireless work
of doctors and nurses
around the world.
In neighbors helping neighbors.
In disconnected families
bonding on Zoom.

In these quiet days,
the world stops in its tracks,
never to be the same.

Everything is changing.

We've been given
the chance
to heal.

Seabirds

Seabirds aloft
in an azure sky.
The bay is calm.
Tiny ripples of understanding
sheltering fears
of what may come.

Greedy politicians
steal from the till.
Our leader
dog-whistles danger
to try and separate
our better angels,
based on the color
of our skin.

As the pandemic
grows exponentially,
the heart of the world
rips in two.

Disparate emotions
run rampant.
Anger, fear, sadness, and compassion
gather . . .
A tsunami
of uncertainty
in this new normal
we've been called
in communion,
to share.

Our grasping,
now upended.
Best made plans,
laid bare.

An eerie quiet buffets
the noise of all
that's inauthentic,
calling us home
to hear
what's most important . . .

To learn to rest
in the present moment
and envision
what together,
we're being summoned
to create.

Will we seize the moment?
Will love triumph over hatred?
Will we recognize
we were made for these times
and do our part,
or shrivel up in fear?

A new era of love
now beckons,
the seabirds
to change course.

Pilgrimage

Red-tailed hawk
soars through gray,
mottled skies.
A quarrel of sparrows follows.

Easter morning silence,
summons
to fly deeper
into the holy font
of broken-hearted
Hope.

Imploring us
to lay down
all assurances,
preoccupations,
even faith,
as humble offerings
to the vast unknown.

Calling the world to bear witness
to the unimaginable suffering,

the devastating weight of sadness,
the heavy atmosphere of grief,
standing sentry.

Its call
entreats the healthy
to release our projects,
our illusions of control,
our plans, priorities,
and expectations
for tomorrow,
and rest in the stillness
of our collective exile.

To reconsider
who we were,
who we are,
and who we are becoming.

Each step,
a prayer,
on this pilgrimage
of pandemic.
Knowing what was
will never be normal.
Holding hope,
with insight and grace,
that who we become
will be better.

The Great Reckoning

Hi Mama,

It's been ten months since I've written. As I think about every-
thing that's happened these past three months, I'm grateful you
left this earth when you departed. COVID is wreaking havoc all
over the world, and everyone's on lockdown.

    Julie and I flew to New York in the middle of February
for some Seva Foundation events and to visit the kids. A few
days after we returned to California, she went to bed with a
headache and debilitating fatigue, but quickly bounced back
two days later. Four days after she got sick, I developed a hor-
rible headache and the worst sore throat I've ever had. That
turned into a respiratory infection that quickly advanced to
pneumonia. I almost had to be hospitalized because my oxygen
levels were so low.

    Now, almost two months later, my lungs are finally clear, and
my energy is returning. Testing was difficult to come by early in
the pandemic, so I didn't get a PCR test until three weeks into
my illness. My test came back negative, but my doctor said she
was 95% sure I'd had COVID based on my symptoms, and it
would have been detected if I'd been tested earlier in my illness.
Despite how sick I've been, I'm one of the lucky ones.

 225

Many times during these past two months, I've thought of you and of how incredibly difficult this pandemic would have been for you to weather. They've locked down all the senior living facilities and aren't allowing visitors. We would have moved you to our house if you'd still been here, but it would have been so hard for you to be away from your daily routine and from all of your friends at Bay Park. Adeline and your other friends must take their meals in their rooms and no one can visit, so it's a lot like being in prison.

The kids had to cancel their spring break trip to visit us in March, and we have no idea when we'll be able to see them. We try and Zoom with them every weekend and play games like hangman, but you can tell that not seeing their friends or being able to go to school is beginning to take its toll.

We were ordered by the county to close down our vacation rental indefinitely, as this virus is so lethal and contagious. Our neighbor Andria has been shopping for our groceries every week since it's too dangerous for me to go into stores and Julie is trying to protect me. We're both working from home, and I'm grateful we both have jobs that allow us to do that. I've been offering meditation classes for one of my clients on Zoom every week. It feels good to be able to provide a space that gives people a place to rest, as everyone's trying to weather this storm the best they can. I'm grateful this is one way I can contribute.

Schools and businesses are shut down, and you have to wear a mask whenever you go outside. Health care workers are stretched quite thin, and many are burning out or getting sick themselves. Every night at eight o'clock, the neighbors go out on our decks and howl to show them support. Andria's sixteen-year-old-daughter, Mia, comes over every two or three days to help us give Roxie the infusions for her kidneys on our patio, which we must time with the rains, since it's unsafe to be inside with anyone except your family.

Mama, so many people are dying, but I'm sure you already know that. Life as we know it came to a screeching halt almost overnight. No one knows if you might be the next one to die.

What comforts me most is knowing if that person is me, then you will be there waiting.

One thing that's happened as a result of the pandemic is how grateful I am you made your exit when you did. This is the last thing I'd ever want you to have to experience. I don't think your mind would have understood it, and you would have been so anxious for us all.

The other day in one of our chats, you told me how there were many angels helping us and sending us light in these terrifying times. You also said that there would be many more people leaving the earth before this was over and to trust the larger plan that was unfolding.

I'm grateful that I now understand how thin the veil is, and that heaven and earth are not such distant places. I'm not afraid to die, but I do want to live now. I just want to be helpful in whatever way I can. If the plan is for me to do that from earth, then I'm very happy to do that. If I'm supposed to do it from heaven, that's fine too. At least I'll have a great teacher when I get there.

Mama, I hope humanity can learn the lessons from this pandemic. That we can find love in our hearts for one another and stop all the hatred that continues to rip us apart. The other day in our chat you said, *"You are living in the midst of the great reckoning now on earth. Everyone is being called to choose a side. Will you choose love, or will you choose hatred? Will you choose hope, or will you choose fear? Every decision each one makes will collectively determine the final outcome. Never forget, my darling, that you always have a choice."*

Mama, I want you to know that I'm doing my best to choose to be a loving person, even when I read or watch the news and am immediately provoked to anger. I'm trying to choose hope, even in those moments when my mind is filled with terror. I'm seeking to focus on peace, even when I experience political fallout around me, and my instinct is choosing war. I am trying to do what you asked me to do, to be an ambassador of love in a broken, angry world.

So, thank you, Mama, for watching over us during these dark days, for sending the angels to guide and protect us, and for helping me heal my lungs so I can breathe again. Thank for you for reminding me I always have a choice to love or strike back, and that the world I see around me is a reflection of those choices. I'm grateful for your continued presence and for being there whenever I need you, especially right now.

I love you and I miss you,

Donna

The Road We Traveled

Every day I think of you,
especially today.
The road we traveled,
treacherous miles
of individuation . . .

Short shorts.
Shaggy bangs.
Not being ladylike.
My "lifestyle."
Sparring over politics.
Wrestling with religion.

Control,
the Colosseum
that contained us.

For most of the years we shared,
we wanted each other
to be the person

we were not.
Our deepest longing,
to learn
to love through
differences,
and find acceptance
as we were.

The last years
of your life
our path became clearer,
less obstructed,
fewer potholes,
more grace.

The landscape opened
as we released
our agendas,
and learned
to mother
one another,
through the balm
of tender care.

The glare
of judgment
removed from our eyes,
finally able to see
the gift we could be
to each another.

The years
that we wasted
in battle,
absolved
by the love,

that one day,
without knowing,
finally
set us free.

Ode to Joy

Bearing the weight
of your loss
for nine hundred days.

Clear-eyed,
and yearning to shed
these ragged old clothes
that have bound us
inextricably
since birth.

Slowly dipping my toes
in the healing waters
of unbridled joy,
like Sisyphus,
I falter.

Afraid releasing the grief
that constrained us
for a lifetime
will make you disappear.

Ready to release the reins
of the oxcart
I've wrestled to pull
up this holy hill,
remove my last
shred of clothes,
and joyfully,
dive in.

Metamorphosis

Hi Mama,

It's been a few months since I've written, but I had the most amazing revelation today that I wanted to share. Two days ago, our neighbors Spencer and Lynn offered us a front row seat to watch the chrysalises from their garden molt into monarch butterflies. While Julie and I walked the dogs this morning, I stopped by to check on the progress of the chrysalises while they were away on vacation. Spencer had hung seven of them from a board at the bottom of the window by the garage, and I noticed one was very close to emerging from her silken cocoon.

I had a number of things on my schedule today, but I followed my intuition, came home, grabbed my camera, camping chair, lunch, and headphones, climbed back up the hill, and waited for the miracle of birth to unfold.

I learned so much in the time I sat there watching the miraculous process of a chrysalis transform into a newly minted monarch butterfly and finally take flight. What I absorbed in seven hours likely would have taken me seven years to discover any other way.

Mama, the first thing I learned was to pay closer attention to the call of my soul and heed its instructions, rather than being held captive to all the things I "should" be doing. Then I won't miss the magic that's unfolding everywhere around me.

The second thing I realized is when it's time to metamorphose and be born into a new form, nature knows exactly what's required, so I don't need to try and control or rush the process. The only thing I have to do is to surrender and enable it to unfold through being willing to listen, observe, and be still. That's something you've been doing your best to try and teach me.

The third thing I discovered is that transformation takes time. It's a two-step forward, one-step back process and requires the faith to trust that it will happen in its own time, instead of trying to force it to occur in a particular way.

I watched that butterfly emerge from a chrysalis that was once a caterpillar, and she was the most majestic creature I'd ever seen. But the journey took time. It took patience. She first had to break free of the cocoon that curtailed any movement. And once free, she needed time to rest, regather her strength, and allow her wings to dry. She had to rid herself of all the excrement she no longer needed to sustain her, then patiently wait as her newly formed wings gradually unfolded, one microsecond at a time.

As the cocoon cracked open, I watched the newly formed creature move in nuanced, finite movements, unfolding herself from a ball into a butterfly, convincing herself that she was capable of flight. Then she stopped and rested before attempting to move again, slowly parting her wings a millimeter or two at a time, then bringing them back together as she allowed the breeze around her to gently move her body—each time, coming back to center as her wings began to harden.

Then very gently, she tested her legs, ensuring they could carry her to the next place that she needed to go. Making certain they were coordinated and could work together, she hung tenuously to the surface of the windowsill where she was standing. What I learned from that part of the process is how important balance and nuance are in our lives, and that it's critical to find our footing before we attempt to fly.

Then slowly and methodically, the newly hatched creature began flapping her wings with greater force while standing still. Then she started to walk, while simultaneously flapping her wings with intention. What I understood is that to fly, we must learn how to balance being earthbound as human beings with our divine nature as spiritual beings. And as we learn to build both of these capacities, ultimately we can travel wherever we're destined to go.

Slowly and methodically, the beautiful monarch butterfly began flapping her wings. Then she'd walk another inch. Then stop again. Then flap her wings. Walk another inch, then stop again. It was a beautiful pattern of rebirth I watched unfold. There was no rush, no sense of impatience, just deep trust that nature knew her next steps. Then willingly, she followed its directions, because everything the strong yet fragile butterfly needed to know was embedded in her DNA.

Each time she flapped her wings, her wingspan grew fuller, more stunning, more whole. But despite all the progress she had made, she wasn't yet ready to launch. But when she reached the end of the windowsill, she had to choose. Would she move forward? Or would she stay where it was safe?

She sat there for forty-five minutes, pondering her next step, not quite ready to make the leap. Deep within, she trusted her instincts, knowing she needed the patience to give herself the time and space to fully harden her wings before she was ready to fly.

Then it began. The long, steep climb up the window, her tiny feet grasping the webbing on the screen. Methodically, diligently, intentionally, for the next half hour, she climbed one foot in front of the other in a vertical trajectory all the way up to the top of the window screen, stopping periodically to flap her wings and remember she was meant to fly.

When she finally reached the frame at the top of the screen, her right front and back feet reached out, and suddenly she realized there was no more footing left to grab onto. The time had come to launch herself. There was no turning back. No option but to fly. With every bit of wisdom encoded in her DNA, she took off, brilliantly flapping her wings. In swirling figure eights, she moved so quickly it was hard to keep her in sight, as she made her first flight across the roses past the birdbath.

She was airborne for fifteen feet before she flew down to the bark in the garden where she stopped for a moment to rest, reveling in what she'd just accomplished. She was no longer a mere caterpillar who could only walk. She was no longer a chrysalis bound who could not move. She was now a beautiful, multicolored monarch butterfly who had the power to fly and make her next migration.

As I reveled in her beauty, I realized that you were the one who sent the butterfly that I'd been observing all day. It was you, in your gentle way, teaching me everything I needed to know about how to break free of my chrysalis of grief and learn how to fly without you.

So, thank you, Mama, for the beautiful lessons today and for hanging out with me in Spencer and Lynn's garden. I sense the time has finally come for me to spread my wings and fly.

I love you and I miss you,

Donna

2021

Roxie's death was such a miracle. I felt your presence everywhere around us. A cylinder of light pulsated around us as a vacuum descended and swept her life force from my arms. As bereft as I feel from her loss, I rest in the faith that the circle of life is unfolding, and that neither one of you are ever far away.

Three Years

Three years have passed
since you opened your eyes
one last time,
and my journey began
here without you.

Three years have passed.
I am not the same
person now
that I was then.

I am stronger,
less fearful,
less anxious,
more secure
of my ground
in the sacred.
More trusting
of its protection.
More reliant
on self-compassion,
mercy, hope, and love.

You are the bridge
that's enabled
my connection
to miracles and mysteries,
both sacred
and mundane.

Your spirit,
strong and revelatory,
always present
whenever needed.
Ever steadfast
in times of doubt.

The bond we formed
in my adolescence
and adulthood
was forged of struggle
and judgment—
Steel grating on granite,
for most
of my lifetime.

But it is soft
and porous now.
The light of love
and devotion
filtering through
the fissures
of healing
we began
in your last years.

Ours is a love story
of forgiveness
and grace,

of deep yearning
to craft the bond
we longed for.

Through our willingness
to forgive and accept,
the love we shared
became grander
than our differences,
our ideologies,
or whom we chose
to love.
As we allowed our hearts
to open,
we welcomed each
other in.

Three years have passed
since you took your last breath.

I still long for the sound
of your laughter
and the touch
of your soft,
gentle hand.

You are woven
into the fabric
of my being now,
Divine Mother of my heart.

Slack Tide

Seagulls soar
above an incoming tide,
mewing Easter blessings.

A sharp soprano chorus
of emergence
from the suffering
and incalculable losses
of three and a half million
mothers, fathers, children,
husbands, wives, and friends,
stolen in thirteen months
of a raging pandemic,
summon us to listen
to its subtle melody
of hope.

A world in limbo
begins to bud.
Calla lilies blossom
as daylight lingers,
and it's deemed safe again
to hug the ones we love.

After you died,
you promised
you would never leave me,
and I could touch your face
in the warm spring breeze,
see the glint of love in your eyes
in the twinkling sky,
watch your spirit soar
in the guise
of a red-tailed hawk,
and feel the warmth
of your touch
in the hand
of my beloved.

Your presence,
in these years
since you've departed,
has never wavered.
Our healing,
never faltered.
Our connection,
only strengthened.

The mother love
in which you've held me
across the veil
through these difficult days
has steadied,
awakened,
and transformed me.

The immeasurable love
you promised
I'd someday find in heaven,
you've showered upon me
on earth.

On this Day of Resurrection,
shedding tears of joy
for the bond we share,
I'm in awe of the depth
of our unwavering connection,
moved by the blessed balm
of forgiveness
to set things right
and make us whole,
and graced by the presence
with which you continue
to hold me,
in the slack tide
of your everlasting love.

Sweet Little Jesus Girl

Hi Mama,

Our house has been a temple of grief the past three days. Yesterday, we had to say goodbye to our sweet little Roxie girl. The only thing that made it bearable was knowing you were there to help me.

When I took her in for her appointment two days ago, the vet told me she was now in end-stage kidney failure and that the most loving thing we could do was to put her to sleep. She assured me we'd given her the best life possible and had extended her lifetime for at least a year through the saline infusions we've been giving her every few days this past year. I came home after our appointment and told Julie the horrible news as we held one another and wept. We both knew this day was coming. We just prayed it wouldn't be so soon.

Yesterday felt interminable as we watched the clock tick down in nauseous anticipation of our 5:30 appointment with Dr. Reed. Julie and I canceled our meetings and took the day off to spend our final day with Roxie. We took her on one last ride on our morning walk in her buggy. Tears of sadness rained down our cheeks as we watched her little silken terrier head bobbing back and forth taking in the familiar sights of her neighborhood one last time.

When we came home, Julie, Bella, Roxie, and I all lay on the floor on blankets in front of the fireplace in the kitchen for the rest of the day. Julie and I took turns snuggling with Roxie. We regaled her with stories of the many ways she'd blessed our lives and told her how grateful we were she'd found us and become such an integral part of our family.

In the middle of the afternoon, Roxie got up from her bed and walked slowly over to Bella's pad. She placed her sweet, angelic face on Bella's back and snuggled up next to her as if to tell her sister how much she loved her, and it was time to say goodbye. Since she ran into Julie's arms that fateful day on Dornan Drive eight years ago, she's always been like Velcro with Bella. For the first time since they've been pack mates, Bella allowed her to stay.

At one point, Roxie hobbled slowly over to the patio door where she always stood next to your feet. She lay on the pad and kept looking out the window as the sun beat down on her face. I had a sense that you were giving her instructions and letting her know you'd be there to take her home when she took her final breath.

Every time I started weeping, I'd leave the room because Roxie was such a sensitive soul, and I wanted her last day on earth to be happy. After you died when I was so bereft, every time I cried, she'd jump in my lap and lick the tears from my face whenever I was sad. I knew you'd given her strict orders to take care of me, because she never left my side for six entire weeks. I don't know if I could have borne the pain if she'd left us while I was still in the depths of my grief. When we thought that she was going to die fourteen months ago, the extra time we got to spend with her was such a special gift.

During one of my meltdowns yesterday as all the grief I felt from losing you came flooding back, I walked downstairs to our bedroom pleading for your help. "Mama," I cried out between sobs, "I really need your help. In a couple of hours, we have to say goodbye to Roxie. For the past two years, she's been my link to you. What will I do without that connection? It feels as if it's fading more and more each day. If you're still there, Mama," I pleaded, "when we take her to the vet to put her down, will you take her from my arms when her sweet little soul leaves her body? I don't want her to be alone or feel afraid."

Your tender voice whispered, *"My sweet, darling girl, I'm so sorry your heart is breaking. I haven't gone anywhere. I'm still with you. Of course, I'll help you. I promise I'll catch Roxie. I love that sweet, precious dog. Her little body has finally worn out and she's in pain. I promise you're doing the right thing for her, sweetie. When you go back upstairs, tell her Nana will be there to take her from your arms when it's time for her to go."*

Then you offered explicit instructions. *"Honey, when you take her to put her to sleep, hold her in your arms exactly like you do when you give her the saline treatments. Let her heartbeat attune with yours. That always calms her, and she knows she's safe in your arms."*

Then you said, *"When the doctor puts the needle in her leg, just hold her tight, radiate love, and surround her with light, and that will help her make her transition. And I'll be on the other side waiting to receive her. Just like I'll be there waiting for you when it's your turn to come Home. Just like my mother was there waiting for me when I left my body. Roxie knows it's time for her to go, sweetheart, so be at peace with that. I promise I'll take care of her for you. And just like when I died and sent you lots of signs and symbols of my presence, she'll do the same for you."*

Mama, the experience of Roxie's death was such a miracle. She lay in my lap, and I held her tightly in my arms just as you'd instructed, while Julie held her head. I focused on attuning with her heartbeat. Anne, our vet, gave her the first injection to calm her, then she told us it might take a few minutes for the second shot to take effect before she'd take her final breath.

But the second Anne administered the final injection, I felt your presence everywhere around us. A cylinder of light pulsated around us as a vacuum-like force descended and swept her life force from my arms.

I turned to Julie, then to Anne, and said, "Mama's here and Roxie's gone. She came to take her, just as she promised me she would." Anne took Roxie's pulse and confirmed that she was dead. We brought Bella into the room so she could smell her sister after she died so she'd understand why she wasn't coming home.

Today, I am gutted. We are all so incredibly sad. But I also feel deep peace knowing that our sweet fur baby's spirit is now there with you. Of that, I have no doubt.

I haven't been able to get out of bed all day, my heart is so heavy with grief. Our sweet Bella, who has a limited tolerance for affection, lay beside me for almost an hour this morning with her big Labrador paw in my right hand to comfort me, just as I imagined Roxie's paw in yours.

I've been thinking all day about how, after you died, until she could no longer climb the stairs, every night at 5:00 like clockwork I'd find Roxie downstairs. She'd be sitting in front of the picture of Jesus we brought from your apartment that now sits on the floor in the corner of our bedroom. It's the same picture that hung in Maw Maw's bedroom that brought me such comfort on the many nights I stayed with her when I was a little girl.

Each night when I'd come down to get Roxie for dinner, I'd find her sitting on her hindquarters with her front paws outstretched, staring at Jesus in the Garden of Gethsemane. It looked like she was praying and receiving instructions from somewhere on high. I always wondered if she was getting her orders from you. Then I'd tell her it was time to say goodbye to Jesus and come upstairs and eat her dinner. That happened every single night until we had to start blocking the stairs for her safety. Now she'll finally get to meet him, and I'm sure you'll be the one to introduce them.

Mama, thank you for being there for us yesterday on one of the worst days of our lives, and for caring for Roxie now as she's cared for me since you departed. As bereft as I feel from her loss, I rest in the faith that the circle of life is unfolding, and that neither one of you is ever far away.

I love you and I miss you,

Donna

Grief Is the Guesthouse

The countdown to loss
is interminable.
Saying goodbye
to those we love,
a part of life,
and love's steep price
we're called to bear
to keep an open heart.

Each tender moment
so precious,
as we navigate
the joys
that color sadness,
the happiness
that leads
to longing
for what was never ours
to hold.

Each precious second,
a tightrope
tethering us

to the memories
that made us,
to the future
we must surrender,
to the present
that holds us
in tow.

Each gentle touch,
a reminder
of our frailty,
of our brokenness,
of this brief moment
we're placed on earth
to live.

Grief is the guesthouse
we inhabit.
Each cupboard,
overflowing,
with the risks we took
to open our hearts
to fully love.

Spring's Rebirth

Grief is not a river to forge,
a mountain to summit,
or a destination
to strive
to move beyond.

It is the gradual unfoldment
of the delicate bud
of new awareness,
the integration
of all things
deeply cherished
and lost,
with the promise
of spring's rebirth.

Grief is not something
to try and push through,
sanitize,
or deny.

It is the heart's way
of expanding its boundaries

to hold more love,
more vulnerability,
more tenderness,
and compassion.

Grief is the gift
that helps us extend
beyond ourselves,
beyond our species,
beyond our ideas
of what's possible.

It shatters the veil
between right and wrong,
between heaven and earth,
between this world
and the next.

Grief is the way-shower
of what's most precious,
and enduring . . .
The peace of the present moment,
and the sheer, immense
Divinity of Love.

The Fourth Thanksgiving

My heart, less tender now.
The scales of a defensive,
hate-ridden world
have slowly returned.
An illusion of protection
I vowed when you died,
I would never allow
to intrude
into the soft space
of rippled grief
that held it open.

Your gentle touch,
always a reminder
of what was good in the world.
Of how love could bridge
distance, ideology, religion . . .
and everything
that separates us
from our true nature—

to be a lighthouse of love
for others,
no matter how flawed
we are.

Some days,
I long for the tears
that fed the ocean of loss.
Tiny tributaries
of memories
of my childhood,
adolescence,
and adulthood—
of the hard-fought battles
we finally won,
once we learned
to accept
and recognize
each other.

As I have drifted
further away
from you
in these past months,
my longing
for your presence
has grown deeper.

My yearning
for who I was
as I piloted
those waters of grief
that broke me
into something new
and made me better,

I now long for,
as much
as I long for you.

And for that wisdom,
on this fourth Thanksgiving without you,
I am grateful.

Walk the Sky

You taught me
how to walk the sky,
to reach higher
for love,
to acknowledge
all that's possible,
when we allow loss
to remake us.

You taught me
how to swim the earth
on amphibious feet,
tiny step by tiny step.
Reclaiming trust
that I could move forward
without you,
wherever that path
unfolds.

You taught me
how to fly higher,
unencumbered

by what you
didn't know
how to offer
when I was a child.
To find my bearings,
when I veered off course,
through the air of grace
that floats
between us
now.

You taught me
that love is the balm
that mends all wounds,
that rights all wrongs,
that restores and heals
across life and death,
heaven and earth—
this world and the next.

You promised me
when you left this earth
that someday,
I'd feel whole again.

I didn't realize then
what I know now,
that you had to leave,
so I could learn
how to give birth
to myself.

Epilogue

Hi Honey,

It's your Mama. I wanted to share something I've learned since I've been in heaven. I think it may come in handy.

Sweetie, the whole point of being on earth is to learn how to open and expand your heart even wider. And all the disappointments, all the suffering, and all the losses you face while you walk the earth are the things that help you carve open an even bigger space for love. Then when you get to your heavenly home, you'll appreciate it more deeply because of all the pain you endured while you were on earth.

I'm so grateful, sweetie, for all the healing we did in my last years. I'm sorry I didn't know how to nurture you the way you needed to be loved when you were younger. I had my own healing work to do. But I want you to know that I did my best with what I knew how to do at the time. I know so much more now than I did then, and I am always here to help you.

Honey, I loved you with all my heart when I was your mother on earth, but that doesn't hold a candle to how much I love you now. It will be the blink of an eye before I see you again, and when that day comes, and you draw your last breath, I will take your hand, just like my mother took mine. Until then, sweetie, get lots of rest, love fiercely, be happy, and most of all, be kind.

I love you now and for all eternity,

Your Mama

The Three Musketeers
"As beautiful as heaven."

Acknowledgments

*I would rather walk with a friend
in the dark, than alone in the light.*

—HELEN KELLER

One of the greatest gifts on this journey was the solace I received from the loving souls who supported me as I navigated the portal of mother loss. Some were long-term friends and family members, and others, recent additions in my life who had experienced the sorrow of saying goodbye to a beloved or suffered the loss of their mothers.

Walking the path with those who are grieving is not for the faint of heart. It calls us to put our needs aside to fix things, lovingly listen, and sometimes just sit and silently bear witness. For all of those who walked beside me on this path, I'm deeply grateful. You have helped me become a more compassionate friend through your example. Your empathy and accompaniment were deeply comforting. The generosity with which each of you shared your personal experiences and provided me with a safe place to grieve helped me heal, and I thank you from the bottom of my heart.

First, to those who helped me care for Mama while she was living in California, I am deeply grateful, especially to Emerald Caregivers, the staff at Bay Park Senior Living, and our friend Pat Carrington. You made my mother's life happier, and ours, less stressful by keeping her entertained, taking her to the doctor when I was working, dispensing medications, and helping her locate the things she often misplaced.

I hold a deep debt of gratitude in my heart for Chaplain Phoebe at Alta Bates Hospital in Berkeley, who Mama was delighted to discover was also a Baptist. Your prayers were like manna from heaven for us all. And to the attentive and caring staff in the ICU, thank you for helping make my mother's transition as comfortable as possible. Especially Dr. Forest Mealey, who sat with us at 3:00 a.m. and compassionately helped me make the toughest decision I've ever had to make.

To my soul friends and teachers who have graced my life and walked beside me through this and other difficult journeys, I could not have done it without you. Thank you, Laura Elliott, Jean Houston, Mary Ann Ireland, Art Libera, Sandra Lommasson, Pauline Reif, and Penny Rosenwasser for your loving care and attention during and after my darkest hours. Your companionship and wisdom are gifts more precious than gold.

And to the staff at Hospice by the Bay in Larkspur, California, who bring so much comfort to departing souls as they prepare to make their transitions, and who help their loved ones find our bearings when they're gone, I'm deeply grateful, especially to my bereavement counselor, Michelle Miller.

To my Holy Darkness, Holy Light and Magus Women's Circle soul sisters who have been with me each step of the way on this journey, including Noreen O'Donnell, Stephanie Weekes, Micki Aaronson, Emma Phillips, True Lucas, Monica Verplank, and Kate Erland, the cord that binds us is eternal. My heart is full of blessings I receive from you every month from bearing witness to your journeys to sharing so freely your wisdom and love.

And to my Avalon family who helped me understand what Mama meant when she said it was possible to discover heaven on earth, thank you for creating the journey that enabled me to pass through the dark portal of grief and experience joy again. Deep gratitude to one and all, especially Lina Berntsen, Katherine Witteman, Brad Laughlin, and Pauline Reif. The journey we shared was the medicine I needed.

To my friends both old and new who helped me on this journey through the She Writes Press Author Group and Facebook who are too numerous to mention, thank you from the bottom of my heart for holding me in your hearts, and for sharing your stories of how you walked the path of letting go.

And to my writing coaches, teachers, and friends Brooke Warner, Linda Joy Myers, Amy Ferris, and Linda Schreyer, thank you for believing in me, for tending my heart when I needed it most, and for helping me improve my craft along the way.

To my beta readers and proofreaders Micki Aronson, Brian Bort, Kate Erland, Rita Hovakimian, Susan Knighten, True Lucas, Julie Nestingen, Emma Phillips, Barbara Stark-Nemon, Kenji Yoshino, and Monica Verplank, thank you for your insights that helped me craft a better book.

And finally, to my family. How blessed I am for your love and support through the years. Especially Karen Shannon and Susan Knighten, my wing-women at Mama's funeral and the closet thing I'll ever have to sisters. I can never express how much it meant to me to know that I could lean on you for support. And to my aunt Nell Berry, Mama's big sister, who has always been my second mother, but after Mama's death, became my first. Thank you for showing me how big the world is when I was a child growing up in West Texas, and for holding my hand through our shared grief.

To my niece and nephew, Sophia and Luke Stoneham-Yoshino, thank you for always bringing a smile to my face and a glow to my heart as you remind me to live in the present moment. You were an unexpected, healing gift to Nana late in her life and have always been the gift that keeps on giving in mine. I love you to the moon and back forever.

And most importantly, to Julie Nestingen, my beloved wife and companion on this journey for thirty-two years, you teach me more about the power of love to heal and make us whole than I ever imagined possible. Your patience and willingness to support me through all the years it took Mama and me to mend our relationship matters more than you can know, especially the times when you were wounded by her comments and could have easily walked away. I could not have emerged on the other side of this portal of grief without your love and tender care. You are the greatest treasure in my life. And in her later years, you proved to be one for Mama. I love you beyond measure and am so blessed to walk this path with you.

About the Author

Donna Stoneham, PhD, is an executive coach, transformational leadership expert, and former hospice chaplain. She was born and raised in the Texas Panhandle but has called Northern California home since her late twenties and now lives with her wife and rescue dogs in Point Richmond, California. Donna is the author of *The Thriver's Edge: Seven Keys to Transform the Way You Live, Love, and Lead* (She Writes Press, 2015) and a featured poet in the anthology *Art in the Time of Unbearable Crisis: Women Writers Respond to the Call* (She Writes Press, 2022). A popular speaker and media guest, Donna's work has been featured in the *Wall Street Journal*, *Woman's Day*, *The Huffington Post*, *TD Magazine*, *Woman's World*, *First for Women Magazine*, *Chispa Magazine*, *Conscious Lifestyle Magazine*, and *Investor's Business Daily*. When she's not writing, coaching, or traveling, she loves to hike, ski, sail, kayak, and commune with spirit and nature. To learn more about Donna and her work, please visit: www.donnastoneham.com and www.positiveimpactllc.com.

Author photo © Chris Loomis

SELECTED TITLES FROM SHE WRITES PRESS

She Writes Press is an independent publishing company founded to serve women writers everywhere. Visit us at www.shewritespress.com.

Soul Psalms: Poems by U-Meleni Mhlaba-Adebo. $16.95, 978-1-63152-012-9. A powerful, lyrical collection of poetry that explores themes of identity, family, love, marriage, body image, and self-acceptance through the lens of a cross-cultural experience.

Unfolding in Light: A Sisters' Journey in Photography and Poetry by Joan Scott and Claire Scott. $24.95, 978-1-63152-945-0. An elegant book of photographs, accompanied by poems, that invite readers to discover the beauty, simplicity, and spirituality that flows through hands.

Benediction for a Black Swan by Mimi Zollars. $14.95, 978-1-63152-950-4. A lush, provocative collection of poems about childhood, children, marriage, divorce, alcoholism, and the sensual world.

Not If, When: Lyme Disease in Verse by Gail Tierney. $16.95, 978-1-63152-735-7. Arranged chronologically in the order that they were written, these autobiographical poems move from devastation to determination, addressing the various frustrations and dynamics of living with chronic Lyme disease—the isolation, the trauma, the fear—and also providing a voice of solidarity and inspiration for those suffering from this devastating illness.

(R)evolution: The Girls Write Now 2016 Anthology by Girls Write Now. $19.95, 978-1-63152-083-9. The next installment in Girls Write Now's award-winning anthology series: a stunning collection of poetry and prose written by young women and their mentors in exploration of the theme of "Revolution."

Times They Were A-Changing: Women Remember the '60s & '70s edited by Kate Farrell, Amber Lea Starfire, and Linda Joy Myers. $16.95, 978-1-938314-04-9. Forty-eight powerful stories and poems detailing the breakthrough moments experienced by women during the '60s and '70s.